Reminiscences of

Rear Admiral Edward K. Walker

U.S. Navy (Retired)

U.S. Naval Institute

Annapolis, Maryland

1985

Preface

A naval career takes a number of unexpected turns during its course from the Naval Academy to retirement, and such was the case with Admiral Walker. As a junior officer in a battleship in the late 1920s, he was designated a "volunteer" for submarine duty and wound up spending the better part of 15 years at it. In that time he commanded the S-21 and made a substantial contribution to the development of the torpedo data computer which played such a large role in the success of fleet submarines in World War II. Because of his extensive knowledge of torpedo fire control, Walker was ironically deprived of command of a fleet boat himself. He was considered more valuable as a member of the Pacific Fleet Submarine Force staff, first in gunnery and fire control and later as operations officer. He served in the latter capacity during the first eight months of World War II. In the memoir which follows, he provides the surprising revelation that knowledge of Ultra, intercepted Japanese radio communication, was so tightly held that even the submarine force operations officer was not informed of it until about May of 1942.

In mid-1942, Admiral Walker's career took another unexpected turn. He was considered too senior to command a submarine and too junior for a submarine division, so he wound up getting command of the destroyer Mayrant. He took her to the North

Africa invasion, convoy duty in the Atlantic, and the Sicily operation. A member of the wardroom in the Mayrant was Lieutenant Franklin D. Roosevelt, Jr. Having the President's son in the wardroom presented a few problems, but most were of the pleasant variety.

After the Mayrant was badly damaged by a German bomb off Sicily, Admiral Walker returned to the United States to serve as a naval ordnance inspector and later commanded an attack transport and two fleet oilers. Subsequently he was a department head at the Naval Postgraduate School, Commander Destroyer Squadron 14, and commanding officer of the Naval Mine Depot in Yorktown, Virginia.

The excellent transcription job of the interviews with Admiral Walker was done by Mrs. Deborah Reid. Admiral Walker has made some changes and corrections to the transcript, but it still stands essentially as he related it during the interviews. Some of the material has been rearranged in sequence in order to provide a smoother chronological narrative, but the substance has not been affected.

                                                   Paul Stillwell
                                                   Director of Oral History
                                                   U.S. Naval Institute
                                                   June 1985

Rear Admiral Edward K. Walker, U.S. Navy (Retired)

Edward Keith Walker was born in Portland, Maine, on 3 October 1904. He attended Portland High School, class of 1921, before receiving an appointment to the U.S. Naval Academy, Annapolis, Maryland. He was graduated and commissioned as an ensign in 1925 and was subsequently promoted in grade until he attained the rank of captain, with a date of rank of 20 July 1943. He was retired from active duty on 1 July 1955, at which time he was promoted to the rank of rear admiral on the retired list.

Upon graduation in 1925, he was assigned to the USS Utah (BB-31), then transferred to the USS Florida (BB-30), serving one year in each battleship, before reporting to the submarine school, Submarine Base, New London, Connecticut, for duty under instruction. He thereafter served consecutively in the USS R-8 (SS-85), R-15 (SS-92), and R-13 (SS-90), attached to Submarine Divisions, Pacific Fleet, based at Pearl Harbor, Territory of Hawaii, until June 1932. He qualified for command of submarines in March 1929. He then had instruction in ordnance engineering at the Postgraduate School, Annapolis, Maryland, continuing under instruction at the Naval Gun Factory, Navy Yard, Washington, D.C.

In the spring of 1935, he returned to duty at sea and served two years consecutively in command of the USS S-21 (SS-126), based at Pearl Harbor, and later in the USS S-31 (SS-136), being decommissioned at the Navy Yard, Philadelphia, Pennsylvania. From January 1938 to June 1940, he was attached to the Bureau of Ordnance, Navy Department, Washington, D.C., and then was assigned to the staff of Commander Submarine Force, U.S. Fleet, for duty as gunnery and torpedo officer, on board the USS Richmond (CL-9), flagship. He remained in that assignment when the command was reorganized as Commander Submarines, Scouting Force, U.S. Fleet, and later as Commander Submarines, Pacific Fleet. In the latter period, from March until August 1942, he was operations and tactical officer. He received a letter of commendation from the Commander in Chief, Pacific Fleet, stating:

"For meritorious conduct in the performance of his duty as Operations and Tactical Officer on the staff of Commander Submarine Force, U.S. Pacific Fleet, from April, 1940 to August, 1942. As a result of his untiring efforts, outstanding ability and energetic initiative in this responsible position, he formulated plans and operational procedures ... which were of tremendous value to the unlimited destruction of the Japanese sea forces ..."

He transferred to duty as commanding officer of the USS Mayrant (DD-402) and served from September 1942 to August 1943 in that command in the European area. He received a letter of commendation with ribbon and combat distinguishing device, from the Secretary of the Navy, stating in part:

"For outstanding performance of duty as Commanding Officer of the USS MAYRANT during the amphibious landings on the Island of Sicily, July 9 to 13, 1943. Skillfully and daringly maneuvering his ship through enemy-infested waters, [he] carried out anti-submarine patrols and provided anti-aircraft defense of transport anchorages off the southern coast of Sicily. Through his fearless initiative and untiring efforts, he enabled his gallant command to furnish such complete protection against hostile attack that our ships were successful in disembarking assault troops and discharging cargo with speed and efficiency ... "

In October 1943 he assumed duty under the Bureau of Ordnance as naval inspector of ordnance at the Ford Instrument Company, Long Island City, New York, and served until 31 August 1945. He received a letter of commendation from the Secretary of the Navy, stating:

"... as Inspector of Naval Ordnance, Ford Instrument Company, New York, during the period from October 2, 1943 to August 31, 1945. Captain Walker was responsible during this period for the manufacture by companies in the New York area of fire control equipment delivered to the Bureau of Ordnance ... "

From October 1945 he served successively in command of the transport Effingham (APA-65) and the oilers Elokomin (AO-55) and Canisteo (AO-99). The latter vessel was assigned to the Navy Antarctic Expedition, 1946-1947, and accompanied the other vessels of the expedition to the area of the antarctic ice shelf. In June 1947, he was ordered to the Navy Department for duty as a member of the joint Army-Navy Explosives Safety Board, and was assigned to the Bureau of Ordnance. The following September he was detached to duty on the staff of the Superintendent, Postgraduate School, at Annapolis, Maryland.

In June 1951 he was ordered to command Destroyer Squadron 14, based in Newport, Rhode Island. He was detached from that duty in June 1952 and ordered to command of the Naval Mine Depot, Yorktown, Virginia. He was retired from active duty on 1 July 1955 with the rank of rear admiral on the retired list.

He transferred to duty as commanding officer of the USS Mayrant (DD-402) and served from September 1942 to August 1943 in that command in the European area. He received a letter of commendation with ribbon and combat distinguishing device, from the Secretary of the Navy, stating in part:

"For outstanding performance of duty as Commanding Officer of the USS MAYRANT during the amphibious landings on the Island of Sicily, July 9 to 13, 1943. Skillfully and daringly maneuvering his ship through enemy-infested waters, [he] carried out anti-submarine patrols and provided anti-aircraft defense of transport anchorages off the southern coast of Sicily. Through his fearless initiative and untiring efforts, he enabled his gallant command to furnish such complete protection against hostile attack that our ships were successful in disembarking assault troops and discharging cargo with speed and efficiency ... "

In October 1943 he assumed duty under the Bureau of Ordnance as naval inspector of ordnance at the Ford Instrument Company, Long Island City, New York, and served until 31 August 1945. He received a letter of commendation from the Secretary of the Navy, stating:

"... as Inspector of Naval Ordnance, Ford Instrument Company, New York, during the period from October 2, 1943 to August 31, 1945. Captain Walker was responsible during this period for the manufacture by companies in the New York area of fire control equipment delivered to the Bureau of Ordnance ... "

From October 1945 he served successfully in command of the transport Effingham (APA-65) and the oilers Elokomin (AO-55) and Canisteo (AO-99). The latter vessel was assigned to the Navy Antarctic Expedition, 1946-1947, and accompanied the other vessels of the expedition to the area of the antarctic ice shelf. In June 1947, he was ordered to the Navy Department for duty as a member of the joint Army-Navy Explosives Safety Board, and was assigned to the Bureau of Ordnance. The following September he was detached to duty on the staff of the Superintendent, Postgraduate School, at Annapolis, Maryland.

In June 1951 he was ordered to command Destroyer Squadron 14, based in Newport, Rhode Island. He was detached from that duty in June 1952 and ordered to command of the Naval Mine Depot, Yorktown, Virginia. He was retired from active duty on 1 July 1955 with the rank of rear admiral on the retired list.

Rear Admiral Edward K. Walker, U.S. Navy (Retired)
Chronological Transcript of Service

July 1921-June 1925	U.S. Naval Academy -- midshipman under instruction
June 1925-June 1926	USS Utah (BB-31) -- assistant second division officer
June 1926-June 1927	USS Florida (BB-30) -- engineering department
June 1927-December 1927	Submarine School, New London, Connecticut -- student under instruction
January 1928-January 1931	USS R-8 (SS-85) -- head of different departments at various times
June 1928	Promoted to lieutenant (junior grade)
January 1931-May 1931	USS R-15 (SS-92) -- engineer officer during decommissioning at Philadelphia
May 1931-June 1932	USS R-13 (SS-90), Submarine School, New London, Connecticut -- gunnery and torpedo officer
June 1932-June 1933	Postgraduate School, Annapolis, Maryland -- student under instruction in general line course
June 1933-June 1934	Postgraduate School, Annapolis, Maryland -- student under instruction in ordnance engineering course
June 1932-June 1935	Naval Gun Factory, Navy Yard, Washington, D.C. -- student under instruction in ordnance engineering at various ordnance facilities
August 1934	Promoted to lieutenant
June 1935-June 1937	USS S-21 (SS-126), Pearl Harbor, Hawaii -- commanding officer
June 1937-December 1937	USS S-31 (SS-136) -- commanding officer

January 1938-May 1940	Bureau of Ordnance, Washington, D.C. -- Fire Control Section, submarine and surface torpedo fire control desk
October 1938	Promoted to lieutenant commander
June 1940-August 1942	Staff, Commander Submarine Force, U.S. Fleet/U.S. Pacific Fleet -- torpedo and gunnery officer; later operations and tactical officer
September 1942-August 1943	USS Mayrant (DD-402) -- commanding officer
December 1942	Promoted to commander
October 1943-August 1945	Ford Instrument Company, Long Island City, New York -- naval inspector of ordnance
September 1944	Promoted to captain
August 1945-October 1945	Damage Control School, Philadelphia Navy Yard -- student under instruction
October 1945-June 1946	USS Effingham (APA-165) -- commanding officer
June 1946-October 1946	USS Elokomin (AO-55) -- commanding officer
October 1946-June 1947	USS Canisteo (AO-99) -- commanding officer
June 1947-September 1947	Army-Navy Explosives Board, Washington, D.C. -- senior Navy member
September 1947-June 1951	Postgraduate School, Annapolis, Maryland -- ordnance curricula officer
June 1951-June 1952	Destroyer Squadron 14, Newport, Rhode Island -- squadron commander
June 1952-June 1955	U.S. Naval Mine Depot, Yorktown, Virginia -- commanding officer
July 1955	Retired from active duty; promoted to rank of rear admiral on retired list

Authorization

The U.S. Naval Institute is hereby authorized to make available to libraries and other repositories of its choosing the transcripts of two oral history interviews concerning the life and career of the undersigned. The two interviews were recorded on 11 and 12 September 1984 in collaboration with Paul Stillwell of the Naval Institute.

The undersigned does hereby release and assign to the U.S. Naval Institute all right, title, restrictions, and interest in these two interviews. The copyright in both the oral and transcribed versions shall be the sole property of the U.S. Naval Institute. The tape recordings of the interviews are and will remain the property of the U.S. Naval Institute.

Signed and sealed this _13th_ day of _Feb_ 1985.

Edward K. Walker
Rear Admiral, U.S. Navy (Retired)

Interview Number 1 with Rear Admiral Edward K. Walker,
U.S. Navy (Retired)

Place: Admiral Walker's home, Glen Rock, New Jersey

Date: Tuesday, 11 September 1984

Subject: Biography

Interviewer: Paul Stillwell

Q: Admiral, to begin at the beginning, could you please tell me what you remember about your parents and your early days in Maine?

Admiral Walker: To go as far back as I remember, we lived at 96 Vesper Street in Portland, Maine. My father was employed as a clerk by the Cumberland County Power and Light Company. I went through the usual schools: kindergarten, primary school, grammar school, and high school. Just before I went to high school, we moved to 39 North Street.

My class in grammar school was a class of change. In other words, the class before me went nine years to secondary school before they went to high school. The class after me went eight years to secondary school before they went to high school. My class went eight and a half years to secondary school before they went to high school. Therefore, I entered high school in January of 1918. And not wanting to spend any more time than I had to in high school, I took extra studies during my high school years, so that I graduated in three and a half years, in June of 1921, from Portland High School.

In the meantime, I had received an appointment to the Naval Academy. At first, I expected to have to take the regular old-fashioned examinations in arithmetic, geography, and so forth, that had been the rule for a number of years at the Naval Academy. So I was going to be tutored by a professor up at Harvard for two or three weeks to get me prepared for those exams. But fortunately, that year they decided that they would permit certification of the top 10% of high school classes to the Naval Academy without any other mental examination. Therefore, the only examination I had before entering the Naval Academy was a physical examination at the Portsmouth Navy Yard to see if it was okay for me to go on to Annapolis.* Of course, after I arrived in Annapolis on July 17, 1921, I took a physical examination there and was sworn in at the Naval Academy as a midshipman in the United States Navy on July 18, 1921.

Stuart Ingersoll lived in the same house that I did at 96 Vesper Street in Portland.** My family had the ground floor. It was what they call a three-flat house. We had the ground floor and his family had the third floor. Stuart was four years ahead of me in school. He graduated from high school in 1917 and went

---
*The Portsmouth Navy Yard is in Kittery, Maine, on the Maine-New Hampshire border.
**Stuart H. Ingersoll was graduated from the Naval Academy in the class of 1921 and eventually rose to the rank of vice admiral. In the mid-1950s he served as Commander Seventh Fleet.

Walker #1 - 3

into the Naval Academy. So I used to go up to his mother's about every month and read The Log that he used to send to her.* And I've known Stuart as long as I can remember. He was always known in the Navy as "Slim." About three years ago, I met him down in Florida on Santa Maria Island. He was there at a motel and I went over to see him, and some other people were with me that knew him. And I called him Stuart. He said, "You're the first person that's called me Stuart since I can remember."

Q: Do you have any other recollections of him?

Admiral Walker: Yes. I remember he was one of the top students in our high school. His mother was very educationally oriented. She'd been a graduate of Oberlin College, and she really worked on him. He got one of the so-called Brown Medals at Portland High School. They were given to the top ten people in the class when they graduated, and he got one of the Brown Medals. A man named Brown gave the money, set up a trust fund.

Q: What are your memories of the World War I period?

Admiral Walker: My first memory of anything in the newspapers and so forth was the big headlines in the Portland paper of the

---

*The Log is a magazine which has been published for many years by Naval Academy midshipmen.

sinking of the _Titanic_ in 1912.* I well remember the start of World War I in 1914. I was that summer selling flowers for my aunt, who raised them, at several of the summer hotels on Peak's Island. And I well remember the start of the war. During the war, I remember especially seeing the Canadian Pacific trains coming into Portland and unloading soldiers to be taken by British ships to Europe, and also British ships coming back with wounded and being loaded on the Grand Trunk railroad for transportation to Canada.

Q: Was there a feeling, since you were so far north, that the United States should get into it at that point?

Admiral Walker: As I remember, people seemed to have the feeling that somehow we were going to have to get into it. That's my recollection. Most people didn't really want to, but they sort of had the feeling that we probably would have to.

Q: Were politics discussed a good bit in your family during those years--for example, the Wilson and Hughes election in 1916?

Admiral Walker: I remember the election and that my family had voted for Hughes, and they were disappointed when Hughes was not

---

*The British White Star liner _Titanic_ sank the night of 14-15 April 1912 as the result of hitting an iceberg in the North Atlantic. Approximately 1,500 died as a result.

elected in 1916.* Yes, I remember that.

Q: Was there a good deal of patriotic fervor in your area?

Admiral Walker: As soon as war was declared, there was definitely a great deal of patriotic fervor. And that lasted up until the Armistice in November of 1918, and I well remember that day. Just how we got the word, I don't remember, because we didn't have any radio. It must have been in the morning paper. I was in high school at the time, and the schools were closed. I remember going downtown and getting on trucks and riding all over town and cheering and waving flags all day long on November 11, 1918.

Q: Was there a sense of relief, then, in the community after that, that it was over?

Admiral Walker: I don't recall it.

Q: Did the war years have anything to do with your desire to get into the Navy yourself?

Admiral Walker: No, I decided when I was fairly young--about

---

*In the presidential election of 1916, the Democratic incumbent, Woodrow Wilson, narrowly won reelection against the Republican challenger, Charles Evans Hughes.

10, 11 years old. I read two books: Dick Prescott at West Point and Dave Darrin at Annapolis, and I decided right then and there I wanted to go to the Naval Academy.*

Q: Why did you pick Annapolis, as opposed to West Point?

Admiral Walker: Well, the seafaring background of my family. My paternal grandfather was a master shipbuilder in Yarmouth, Maine. My maternal grandfather, along with three other brothers, owned and operated a salt fish business where they sent the vessels to fish for cod off the Grand Banks and brought them into Portland harbor and sun-dried them on weirs on House Island.**

Q: Had you been boating at all or been to sea yourself before then?

Admiral Walker: No. No.

Q: So it was a combination of these books you read and the family background that pushed you toward Annapolis.

---
*The Darrin series comprised four novels for boys, each one covering one of the four years in the Naval Academy course. Dave Darrin's First Year at Annapolis was published in 1910 and the other three in 1911. H. Irving Hancock was the author of the series; all four books were published by the Saalfield Publishing Company of Akron, Ohio.
**The Grand Banks is the name of an area in the Atlantic south and east of Newfoundland, Canada.

Walker #1 - 7

Admiral Walker: That is correct.

Q: How did you go about getting the political appointment?

Admiral Walker: One of the backers of the representative from our district was a very good friend of my father's, and he and my father were quite prominent in our church; his name was H.F. Merril. He arranged with this representative that if he was elected, he would appoint me to the Naval Academy.* And there again, there was a slight slipup. I had asked for appointment to the class of 1926, because I didn't expect to graduate until '21 and I thought I'd need a year to get prepared for the Naval Academy examinations. What the Naval Academy wanted I had studied way back when I was in grammar school. But the representative made a mistake and appointed me to the class of 1925, and, fortunately, I didn't have to take any mental examinations.

Q: Do you think you would have had problems with those?

Admiral Walker: No, I don't, but I mean, you know, I was rusty on arithmetic and geography and that sort of thing. The other things, no problem at all, English and history and that sort of

---
*Carroll L. Beedy, Republican of Portland, Maine, was elected a member of Congress from the state's first district in the election of September 1920.

Walker #1 - 8

thing. But mostly arithmetic and geography. I had been through algebra and geometry and trigonometry already in high school. But I forgot all my arithmetic.

Q: You must have been a pretty diligent student to be able to complete the course in three and a half years.

Admiral Walker: I was a good student. I stood better than the top 10% of my class in high school. I think I was somewhere around 12 or 15 in my class, something like that.

Q: Out of how many, approximately?

Admiral Walker: We graduated about 330.

Q: I'd say you did do well.

Admiral Walker: Yes, yes.

Q: Did you have any teachers there in school who particularly inspired you?

Admiral Walker: Yes, I had one, a history teacher, a woman by the name of Miss May Tolman, and I had a Latin teacher, Chippy Morse, who'd also been my mother's Latin teacher in high school.

I had another woman teacher in mathematics, whose name I can't recall now. She was excellent, too.

Q: Were your parents interested in you getting a good education?

Admiral Walker: Oh, definitely. They weren't very well to do, and they didn't know how they were going to swing it, but they were just convinced my twin sister Ruth and I should get a college education, as neither one of them had one. My father died in 1927, several years after my sister graduated from high school. In the meantime, she had gone to Colby College, and she went two years to Colby College, and then she took a year out to teach Latin in the high school in Elliot, Maine, to get some more money. She finished her last two years at Boston University and graduated, majored in Latin at Boston University. (She died in 1977.)

Q: Your parents were then grateful, I guess, that this opportunity came along to go to the Naval Academy.

Admiral Walker: Oh, very much so. Very grateful, because they knew how badly I wanted to go, and in those days, there was practically no competition or examination, at least up in Maine. It was who you knew to get you an appointment.

Walker #1 - 10

Q: Were there quite a few people trying to get the appointments?

Admiral Walker: I never knew. I never knew. As a matter of fact, there were about five boys from Portland in the class of '24, and I was the only one from Portland in the class of '25. There was another classmate of mine from Yarmouth, Maine. His father was the principal of the high school in Yarmouth, Maine. Then there was another boy came from mid-state somewhere, and another one from Bangor. Let's see. At that time, Maine had two senators and four representatives, and they could appoint at least one every year. They were allowed five in the Naval Academy, at any one time, each senator and representative.

Q: Had you been to the navy yard at Portsmouth there before you got the physical?

Admiral Walker: Never.

Q: What are your recollections of that experience?

Admiral Walker: There's only one thing I remember. I seemed to go along all right until the examination was over. Then the doctor said to me, "If you were going to be appointed to West Point, I wouldn't pass you, because you have a tendency toward flat feet." Isn't it strange, the things you remember? That's

Walker #1 - 11

the only thing I remember about the examination.

Q: What do you remember about the beginning of plebe summer down in Annapolis?

Admiral Walker: My strongest recollection of plebe summer in Annapolis was that when I first went in, I was at a table almost by myself. There were pitchers upon pitchers of milk, and we could just take all the milk we wanted, and I thought that was wonderful, because I had always loved milk. I just remember the usual things, going out in the whaleboats, racing in the whaleboats, some sailing in the half-raters, learning the standard drill at that time. And I remember the awful job of marking all my clothes, getting them at the midshipmen's store and dragging them up to the room and then marking them all and then putting them away in the prescribed manner in the lockers.

Q: Did you have any trouble adjusting to the discipline at the Naval Academy?

Admiral Walker: No, none whatsoever. I was never homesick a moment. I've never been homesick in my life. I don't understand the word.

Q: Was there any hazing on the new plebes?

Walker #1 - 12

Admiral Walker: Not during plebe summer, because there were no upper classmen around. But there was plenty of it during plebe year. There was one great big so-and-so. If I saw him today, I'd still hit him over the head with a baseball bat.

Q: What was his specialty?

Admiral Walker: He liked to beat my rear with a broom while I held my ankles with my hands. He was a crew man. I had been a crew man, too, during my plebe summer, but I wasn't good enough to make the regular plebe crew, so later in the fall, I sort of lost interest and didn't pursue it at all. I didn't row any more until my first class year when they instituted class crews. I rowed in the class crew my first class year, and we won the race on a very rough day. We all were swamped at the finish line, I remember that.

Q: Why did you have that period in between that you didn't do it?

Admiral Walker: I didn't have too much interest in athletics, never did. I knew I wasn't very good, so I spent most of my odd time reading and playing bridge and so forth.

Q: What sorts of things were you interested in reading?

Admiral Walker: Oh, I was an avaricious reader of anything and everything. I always loved history, and naval history was interesting, although I didn't get too many books from the library. I was mostly reading the _Cosmo_ and things like that. During my years in grammar school, I completely read through the _Books of Knowledge_.

Q: Much different from today's _Cosmopolitan_ magazine, I'm sure.

Admiral Walker: Oh, yes, that's right. And _The Saturday Evening Post_ and stories in there. That's the sort, just light reading. I wasn't trying too much to improve my mind. I was just passing the time away. We played a lot of bridge when we could have the time, but plebe year, no. This is when I was an upperclassman. Plebe year was sort of rough, although I was in some ways better off than some of the other plebes. Because the first roommate assigned to me was a man by the name of John Orr from Tennessee, and he bilged out the middle of plebe year. So they assigned another man by the name of J.M. Miller as my roommate, and he had been originally a member of the class of 1923 and had bilged out.* So when any '23 man came into our room and Miller was there, he never bothered me. So I was only bothered in the room by the first class and the youngsters. However, this guy that

---

*Midshipman John Mendelssohn Miller, USN, who was graduated with the class of 1925.

used to beat my tail all the time, he was of '23. I stood just in back of him in ranks all the time. He was always picking on me. I don't know why. He seemed to like to. He had me come to his room for my chastisement.

Q: What did you have to do, just grin and bear it in that situation?

Admiral Walker: Right. Grab your ankles while he'd beat your tail about two or three times a week.

Q: Weren't there official regulations against that sort of thing?

Admiral Walker: Oh, sure. Oh, yes. As a matter of fact, Schuyler Pyne was turned back for hazing, as I recall.* He was '24.

Q: Admiral Eller mentioned that one thing that he enjoyed reading was the Henty series. Did you read those books?

Admiral Walker: Yes. I don't remember the names of the books, but I

---

*Midshipman Schuyler N. Pyne, USN, who eventually rose to the rank of rear admiral as an engineering duty officer. His oral history is in the Naval Institute collection.

remember the Henty name.*

Q: Did any of the course work give you any particular trouble?

Admiral Walker: No, not particularly. I was only on the weekly tree once in the whole four years, and that time we went to a lecture in English in the old lecture hall, and we were supposed to turn in a theme and I forgot mine, so I got a zero for that day. So that gave me about a 2.0 or 2.1 for the week, and that's the only time in the whole four years I was ever on the tree.** I graduated number 58 in my class of approximately 450, and I was commissioned number 50.*** The discrepancy resulted from people who got out for physical reasons or something, or who went into the Marine Corps. We were allowed 25 men to go into the Marine Corps in those days.

Q: Would you say that the studies were pretty easy for you, then?

---

*George A. Henty was an English writer who wrote a series of adventure novels in the 19th century. They were aimed at boys and used the device of having a young hero accompanying a noted historical figure. Rear Admiral E.M. Eller, a Naval Academy classmate of Admiral Walker's, describes the Henty series in his oral history.
**Being "on the tree" meant that an individual had failed to compile a passing mark of 2.5 for the week's work.
***There were 448 graduates in the Naval Academy's class of 1925.

Walker #1 - 16

Admiral Walker: In general, I was lucky in a way. I'd already had three years of French in high school, and when they ask you to make your choice of either French or Spanish, well, I'd had French, so I chose Spanish. But then the officer who was taking our desires and so forth, said, "You boys who have had either French or Spanish, I would strongly suggest that you take it here, because that will give you more time for your math and engineering and English and so forth." So I shifted back and was in the French battalion for my four years at the Naval Academy. There were two subjects I had a little trouble with. One was mechanical drawing. It seems to me I'd just get a beautiful drawing and start to ink it, and I'd make a splotch. And the other was chemistry. I never had chemistry in high school. I'd had physics, but I never had chemistry, and I had a little trouble with chemistry. I can remember one night going to the head about midnight and sitting up studying until 2:00 or 3:00 o'clock in the morning hoping the DO wouldn't come around while I did last-minute studying for a chemistry exam at the end of the quarter, end of the half year, whatever it was.* And I finally passed all right, but I was awfully glad to get rid of chemistry.

Q: I hear there was a guy named Red Magruder that was tough on that.

---

*The DO was the duty officer, who would put midshipmen on report if he found them out of bed after taps.

Walker #1 - 17

Admiral Walker: Oh, he was very tough, yes, yes, Red Magruder.*

Q: Do you recall anything specific about him?

Admiral Walker: No, except that we gave him a silence one morning at breakfast, and that flew around like wildfire. I remember we got to engineering class that morning, and the first thing the officer that was our instructor remarked upon was that he'd heard that we had given Red Magruder a silence.

Q: Was there any kind of a retaliation for doing that?

Admiral Walker: No, not that I recall. I thought there might be, but I don't recall any.

Q: How did the silence work?

Admiral Walker: Well, if you were ever in the mess hall at mealtime, especially in the old one before they had the acoustic ceiling, it was a bedlam, what with the noise of the cutlery and everybody talking. That morning we all came in, sat down, and not a word was said. Absolute silence. You could hear a pin drop in that whole mess hall. It was really something very

---

*Lieutenant Commander Cary W. Magruder, USN.

effective. I still recall it.

Q: And Magruder, I take it, had the duty that day?

Admiral Walker: There was a head duty officer; then there were a couple of duty officers at the main table. To give Magruder a silence, he must have been the head duty officer that day, yes. But he wasn't my battalion commander. He was a battalion commander in the fourth battalion, and I was in the second battalion. I started out in the fourth battalion, spent two years in the fourth battalion, and then at the end of youngster year, they took and shifted the second battalion and the fourth battalion. Of course, in those days, there were only the four battalions. There were two wings that go out back and the two wings out front, in the main building. And as you looked at Bancroft Hall, on the left side was the first battalion, and behind that in the wing was the second battalion. To the right, it was the third battalion and behind that in the wing was the fourth battalion. And I started out in the fourth battalion and ended up in the second battalion. But you could only take one of two languages. You had your choice, French or Spanish. Period.

Q: How was something like that silence organized?

Admiral Walker: Word of mouth. You know, the grapevine.

Walker #1 - 19

It's remarkable how a thing like that can get organized. The details of it, of course, I don't really remember, but I just remember we all got the word. And I don't remember what the trigger was that started it off. I just have completely forgotten what the trigger was.

Q: The Superintendent was Henry B. Wilson.* What do you recall about him?

Admiral Walker: I recall that he always appeared to me to typify a naval officer. He was a very meticulous dresser, he had a jaunty way of wearing his cap, and his white hair. He just looked like an admiral.

Q: I gather also he was a father figure for the midshipmen.

Admiral Walker: Yes, he was. He was a father figure, and we had a captain as Commandant of Midshipmen. He was supposed to have been a hotshot, but he retired about the time we graduated.**

Q: What about Nulton?

---
*Rear Admiral Henry B. Wilson, USN, Superintendent of the Naval Academy from July 1921 to February 1925.
**The Commandant was Captain Harold E. Cook, USN.

Walker #1 - 20

Admiral Walker: Nulton was no father figure at all.* For my money, he was sort of a nonentity. He came in about the middle of our first class year, as I recall.

Q: Could you describe the ceremony in which you all went over the seawall?

Admiral Walker: Yes. At the end of second class year, they had a ceremony at the Naval Academy which had been going on for a number of years. After the second classmen received their rings, they all went down to the seawall and pushed each other over the seawall into the Dewey Basin. In Dewey Basin were tied up a large number of half-raters--in other words, small sloops. And two or three of the sloops had been removed to make space for the midshipmen to jump in. As I recall, there wasn't too much consideration being given for getting the people out of the water, and I was a fair swimmer but not a really strong swimmer. And I started to tire a little, so I swam over to one of the half-raters and held onto the bow for a while to rest myself. Well, a number of the other midshipmen apparently were in the same boat that I was, because they were all climbing aboard these half-raters. And we got too many on one side and she capsized, and a classmate of mine by the name of L.R. Smith was caught

---

*Rear Admiral Louis M. Nulton, USN, Superintendent from February 1925 to June 1928.

under the sail and was drowned.* And after that, there was no more baptizing of the rings in the Severn River. I will never understand why they permitted the sails to be up drying that day.

Q: Were there any of your professors that you particularly remember?

Admiral Walker: Yes. Professor Fournon in French.** He was known as "the aristocrat." He always wore gray suits and a gray fedora hat, gray spats, and carried a cane, and he held himself very well. He was known to the midshipmen as "the aristocrat." Ever heard of him?

Q: No, I haven't. I have heard of C. Alphonso Smith.***

Admiral Walker: That's right, I remember him very well. He had a son who was a little bit younger than we midshipmen, and he used to play around a lot with the midshipmen on the tennis courts and that sort of thing. And then I think he finally went to the Naval Academy. I'm not sure, but as I recall it, he did. He was an outstanding man, C. Alphonso Smith.

Q: Professor Alden was there at the time.

---
*Midshipman Leicester R. Smith, USN, died on 28 May 1924.
**L.R. Fournon.
***Professor of English; head of the English department during the early part of Walker's time as a midshipman.

Admiral Walker: Professor Alden, yes.* He was very good. I remember him. I guess the staff was less than 50% civilians, more naval officers. One of the naval officers I remember well was Admiral Holloway.

Q: Oh, really?

Admiral Walker: Yes. He was a character, even at that time. He was a lieutenant then.**

Q: What do you recall about him?

Admiral Walker: I just recall he was a character. I think we took naval justice and so forth under him, studied old "Rocks and Shoals" under him.***

Q: He was certainly no lawyer, so I guess that wasn't a prerequisite.

Admiral Walker: No, absolutely not. He was no lawyer, that was for sure. Then, of course, he became Superintendent of the Naval Academy, and his son was CNO.

---
*Professor Carroll S. Alden, chairman of the English department after C. Alphonso Smith.
**Lieutenant James L. Holloway, Jr., USN, later a four-star admiral.
***"Rocks and Shoals" was the popular nickname for the Articles for the Government of the Navy, which were in effect from 1862 to 1951.

Q: "Slipstick Willie" was there.

Admiral Walker: Oh, God, I'm glad you reminded me. "Slipstick Willie," he was a real, real character, and the shows he used to put on with his Leyden jars making lightning and everything.* They were just mind-boggling. It would really fascinate the midshipmen.

Q: Did you generally enjoy classes?

Admiral Walker: Yes, I did.

Q: That kind of a system found out for sure whether you had done your homework or not.

Admiral Walker: Oh, yes, you had to recite in every subject, every day. You never had a chance to slip, and you didn't get but very little help from the professor. If you asked the professor a question, he'd say, "Read the book. It's all in there."

Q: Did you think that was a useful method of instruction?

---

*Earl W. Thomson of the electrical engineering and physics department. He got his nickname from his frequent use of the slide rule.

Walker #1 - 24

Admiral Walker: I think it's the best thing that ever happened to me.

Q: Why?

Admiral Walker: I found out during the war my biggest trouble with reserve officers was they couldn't read, write, or understand the English language. You'd give them an operation order to be read.

They'd come back to you and say, "What does it say?"

I said, "For God's sake, what does it say? Read it! It's perfectly plain what it says." They'd been spoon-fed so much by their professors in college, they'd never learned how to read and understand the printed word. That was my biggest problem with reserve officers during the war.

Q: What do you recall of the summer training cruises?

Admiral Walker: My first cruise was in the *Delaware*. She was built around 1908.* We went down in the Caribbean and we stopped at Martinique and St. Thomas. We also stopped at Panama, and then we went on up to Halifax. My big memory of Halifax was that I had loaned my razor to a friend of mine, and when I got it back

---

*Construction of the *Delaware* (BB-28) began in November 1907. She was launched in February 1909 and commissioned in April 1910.

and shaved, I got the barber's itch. So when I got to Halifax, my face was all sore from this barber's itch. And I didn't get to shore at all in Halifax, I looked so badly. One of the ships of the practice squadron was the USS *Olympia*, Admiral Dewey's flagship at Manila Bay. I believe she was decommissioned at Philadelphia.*

On that first midshipmen's cruise, I was the first loader in a turret, and the turret officer was George L. Russell in '21, and he was a relatively new ensign at the time. As first loader, it was my job to push the bags of powder in the breech after the shell had been rammed home. There were two loaders, the first loader and the second loader. The first loader pushed in the first bag; the second loaded pushed in the second bag. The first loader then pushed in the third bag that came up, and the second loader pushed in the fourth bag, and then the gun captain closed the breech. Then the first loader was on the outboard side of the turret, stood back, and he had a couple of handles he could hold onto to keep him steady from the gunfire. I'll never forget the sensation I had when that great big breech of that gun went by me at about I don't know how many miles an hour 'til it hit the end of its run.

---
*The cruiser *Olympia*, first commissioned in 1895, was the flagship of Commodore George Dewey during the victory over the Spanish in the Battle of Manila Bay on 1 May 1898. She was in and out of commission a number of times before her final service training midshipmen in the summer of 1922. She was decommissioned at Philadelphia 9 December 1922. She is now a memorial ship in that city.

Q: How close did it come?

Admiral Walker: About a foot from my stomach. What a sensation that was!

Q: So they needed thin people in that job.

Admiral Walker: They sure did. I was thin in those days. When I entered the Naval Academy, I was my present height, 6'2", but I only weighed 155 pounds. By the end of my plebe year, I was up to 175 pounds, and I weighed that for the next ten or 15 years.

My second class cruise was on the North Dakota, which was the sister ship of the Delaware, and I started out in the engineering department as a fireman. The new youngsters were the coal passers. They went and got the coal out of the bunkers and brought it in, dropped it on the floor plates between the boilers. You generally had four boilers in the fireroom, two facing forward, two facing aft, and the coal was on the floor plates between the boilers. So that's what I had done when I was in engineering in the Delaware. In the North Dakota, I had graduated, so I was a fireman. So I fired the boiler for four hours on and eight off for 17 days from Annapolis to Copenhagen. We really got an education.

We had only been in Copenhagen about 48 hours when we got word we were going to Goteborg, Sweden. There was some sort of a festival for an international holiday going on up there. They wanted a ship of the practice squadron up there, so they sent the North Dakota to Goteborg. Then we went from there to Greenock, Scotland, which is the port for Glasgow. We took trips up through the Trossachs and Loch Louise, and also to Edinburgh, where I toured Edinburgh Castle. And then from Glasgow we went to Gibraltar, and from Gibraltar, back home.

Now, on the first class cruise, I was in the USS New York. I don't remember doing any engineering duty in there, but they had a system then with the first class to teach us navigation. We were assigned to a navigation group for about ten days, and we'd do a full day's work as a navigator every day. And our instructor and boss was "Mick" Carney.* I remember well working with him. I thought that, "Gee, what a wonderful guy this is." I liked him very much, even as a first class midshipman.

Q: What was it about him that impressed you?

Admiral Walker: I don't know. He just seemed to understand midshipmen and their problems and how they operated. He was helpful when he needed to be, and he'd tell us off when we needed to be told off. All of us just liked him, a great guy. Did you interview him?

---

*Lieutenant Robert B. Carney, USN, taught navigation at the Naval Academy from 1923 to 1925. He later served as Chief of Naval Operations from 1953 to 1955.

Walker #1 - 28

Q: No, I've met him but haven't interviewed him.

Admiral Walker: He's still alive, you know, that old rascal. He must be at least 88 or 89, because he's at least ten years older than I am, and I'll be 80 in three weeks.*

Q: He was class of 1916.

Admiral Walker: That is correct. I was almost the baby of my class, and he was the baby of his class. There were only three or four men in my class younger than I am, and for years there wasn't an officer in the Navy that was younger than I who was senior to me.

Q: That's what getting through school in three and a half years will do for you.

Admiral Walker: Yes. In the New York, we went to England that summer.

Q: That would have been the summer of '24.

Admiral Walker: The summer of '24, right. When did Harding die?

---

*Admiral Carney was born 26 March 1895.

Q: '23.

Admiral Walker: '23. To go back a little, I can remember very well, I was sleeping on top of a turret in Gibraltar one afternoon when they lowered the flag to half-mast and the word came through that President Harding had died.* It was my second class cruise.

On the first class cruise, we went to England. I forget the port now in South England that we were in. We got five days to London. There again--this seemed to happen strangely--they had a system that for about ten days or two weeks, groups of first classmen would live in the junior officers' quarters. Most of the junior officers had been detached, and so there were quarters available in the junior officers' quarters, and then we'd eat in the junior officers' mess. And it happened that I was assigned to that group the day before we were to go to London. I woke up the next morning, and I could hardly see, because my eyes were so swollen up by being bitten by bedbugs. I seemed to run into those kind of things.

Then from England, we went to France, and we got five days in Paris. I know we had a very pleasant five days in Paris. Originally, some of us had signed up to stay in a French barracks, because they were going to let us stay awfully cheap. Well, we got there, and we found there were straw

---
*President Warren G. Harding died in office on 2 August 1923.

mattresses in the beds, and we didn't want any part of it. But then the colonel wouldn't let us out. We had to go to the ambassador to get him to contact the ship and get an okay from the admiral to release us from this place so we could find our own place to live.

I remember we went to the Follies Bergere one night, and we met the English troupe, the dancing girls they had. We met them after the show. The next couple of days, we were out with them a lot during the day. We used to go swimming with them in the swimming pool they went to in the Seine. We had a lot of fun in Paris.

Then from Paris, we went to Gibraltar again, and there we had to coal the ship. And they fed us, gave us some Welsh coal that was awful powdery. And I can remember being down in the bunkers, leveling out the coal as it came down the chutes into the bunker. We had gauze over our faces, but even then, you almost smothered to death down there. It was just awful. I've never experienced anything like it in my life, just terrible.

Then each cruise generally we'd come back and have target practice in the Chesapeake Bay before the cruise ended. But in general, I thoroughly enjoyed my cruises.

Q: Did you decide that you were going to enjoy being in the Navy?

Admiral Walker: Yes, I did.

Walker #1 - 31

Q: I take it you had increasing levels of responsibility as each year passed in these cruises.

Admiral Walker: That's right. That is correct. Yes, that's the way they worked it. When you are on deck, you'd be like an ordinary seaman, and, say, the second class cruise, you'd be like a second class petty officer, the equivalent of a second class or first class petty officer. And then on your first class cruise, instead of wearing the roundish looking hat, you wore your regular cap, and you had like junior officer responsibilities on that cruise. So you fleeted up as the cruises went along.

Q: Were these cruises useful in showing you how hard the enlisted men worked?

Admiral Walker: Oh, yes, because we had to do most of the work. They cut the crew in half, and we did all the work that they did. We swabbed the decks; we holy-stoned the decks; we shined the brass; we did everything. On youngster and second class cruise, we were supposed to sleep in hammocks. That presented two problems; the hammocks got dirty and had to be scrubbed, and I almost fell out of mine one night. So I put my mattress and my hammock back in my locker to keep them clean. Then I slept with a blanket on deck, on a steel deck, because that was a lot easier than scrubbing a hammock.

Q: Were there any ships' officers that you recall other than Carney?

Admiral Walker: On the cruise, you mean?

Q: On any of those cruises, or at the Academy.

Admiral Walker: Yes, there's one I can recall very well, and he was killed at Pearl Harbor, and I'm trying to think of his name. He was a captain. I think he was the captain of the Arizona.

Q: Van Valkenburgh?

Admiral Walker: That's it, Van Valkenburgh.* He was an instructor in engineering. I well remember, he invited any one of us that would like to come over any Saturday afternoon or Sunday afternoon and have drinks and cookies, but none of us would go, because that would be being greasy to do that, so none of us went.**

Q: That was frowned on among midshipmen, I take it.

Admiral Walker: Yes, because you're, in effect, greasing up your

---
*Lieutenant Commander Franklin Van Valkenburgh, USN.
**"Greasy" was Naval Academy slang for apple-polishing or seeking to curry favor with seniors.

professor. So that was frowned upon. The same way, it was frowned upon generally going to the Superintendent's receptions. He had two or three of those a year. As a plebe, you always had to go at least once or twice. You got ordered by the first classmen one to go. But by not going you were stupid, because that's where you met all the Navy junior girls, you know. I listened to this thing, and I didn't find out until I was a first classman that I was stupid.

Q: How much of a social life did you have in Annapolis?

Admiral Walker: Well, quite a bit as a first classman, because as first classmen, we were allowed out every afternoon and Saturdays and Sunday. As a plebe, we could only be out Saturday afternoon and Sundays. As a youngster and as a second classman, we could only be out on Wednesday afternoon, Saturdays, and Sundays. But as first classmen, we could go to town every afternoon after classes were over, as long as we were back by dinner time. We generally had physical instruction and exercise in gymnasium Saturday morning, but after noon formation, we could go out. We had all Sunday after chapel, because we all had to go to chapel in those days. You didn't have any choice; you had to go to chapel.

I remember one fellow said he was a Mohammedan, so the duty officer got him a little prayer rug. He said, "All right, I want

Walker #1 - 34

to see you face Mecca every day. Get down on your knees and pray."

Q: Were the midshipmen generally helpful to each other on studies?

Admiral Walker: Yes, in general, they were. My roommate wasn't a particularly good student, but he wasn't particularly bad. I don't remember having helped him very much, but I did a little once in a while, especially in the math and so forth, and sometimes in the French. I really didn't have any problem at all with the French, having had three years in high school. And you had to take three years at the Naval Academy, so I wasn't much ahead of where I left high school when I graduated.

Q: What courses turned out to be most useful for you during your commissioned period, that is, the things that carried on?

Admiral Walker: Well, engineering, navigation, and ordnance, I'd say, offhand. I never did anything much with mechanical drawing. Of course, English is always important. But somehow, English is never popular with students. I don't know why, but generally it isn't, especially with those mechanically or scientifically inclined. It's too bad, because if you don't know how to write and read and talk, well, you're out of luck. I don't do too well these days. Just the word I want leaves me, which is unfortunate.

Q: Who were some of your fellow midshipmen from that period that you particularly remember?

Admiral Walker: One is Butch Parker.* He was a classmate of mine, also in my battalion. So was this friend of mine from Yarmouth, Maine, Dinty Moore.** Another one became comptroller of one of the big insurance companies, or treasurer, I guess, Rosey Ross.*** Another one in there was a boy by the name of Graubart, we called him "Cupie."**** He had a little round face, a little hair that stuck up on the top of his head, so we called him Cupie Graubart. (After graduation, his name became "Speed.") I also well remember J.B. (Jack) Poor; R.A. Guthrie; Kirby Smith Howlett, who resigned on graduation and became a doctor; Ergs Hoag, who was my roommate plebe summer.***** Judge Eller and Dwight Allgood were also in my battalion.******

---

*Midshipman Edward N. Parker, USN, now a retired vice admiral.
**Midshipman Carlton H. Moore, USN, who eventually retired as a lieutenant commander.
***Midshipman Delbert A. Ross, USN, who resigned from the service as an ensign.
****Midshipman Arthur H. Graubart, USN, who eventually retired as a captain.
*****Midshipman Leslie F. Hoag, USN.
******Midshipman Ernest M. Eller, USN. Eventually a rear admiral on the retired list, Eller's oral history is in the Naval Institute collection.

Walker #1 - 36

My company commander first class year was Clifton Grimes.

Q: Parker eventually became a three-star admiral.

Admiral Walker: That is correct.

Q: What do you recall about him?

Admiral Walker: I never really went around with him or went out with him on liberty or anything. I just recall that he was a real nice guy. Now, as a sequel to that, a friend of both his and mine, Thompson Hampton Mitchell, had to retire shortly after we graduated. They thought he had TB.* He went to work for RCA and eventually became president of RCA Communications. Well, shortly after I retired and was working in New York, he asked me if I would like to help him take his boat to Florida. He had a 44-foot Chris Craft, so I said, "Sure, I'd be delighted." Well, it seems that the other member of the crew was Butch Parker. So here was this classmate of ours who had resigned. He had a vice admiral for a bow hook and a rear admiral for a stern hook, and we took his boat from Annapolis to Pompano. That was in the spring. The following fall, we all flew to Florida and brought

---

*TB--tuberculosis, which was then a much-dreaded contagious disease. Mitchell resigned from the Navy in 1927 to join RCA. During World War II, he was commissioned in the Army Reserve to serve in the Signal Corps. He was eventually a colonel.

Walker #1 - 37

the boat back to Annapolis. So I got to know Butch pretty well, because it took us 13 days to go down and 11 days to come back. We had fun. I enjoyed it.

Q: Parker had an unusual nickname, I think you mentioned.

Admiral Walker: Oh, yes--"Cherub."

Q: And why was that?

Admiral Walker: Well, because he was pink-faced and round-faced. He looked like a cherub.

Q: Did you have any disciplinary difficulties while you were at the Academy?

Admiral Walker: No, no. Oh, I'd get put on report once in a while for lint on my uniform or some other crazy thing. No, I never had any major difficulties at all.

Q: You didn't get sent to the ship.*

Admiral Walker: No, no, never got sent to the ship. I'll never

---

*The former Spanish warship <u>Reina Mercedes</u> was station ship at the Naval Academy and also a place of confinement for midshipmen who accumulated too many demerits.

forget, my first class year, I was getting somewhere around 3.0, 3.2 in grease, which was your aptitude for the service mark. So I went down to see the company commander, Lieutenant Commander Cheadle, and I said, "How come? When I don't get any demerits, I only get a 3.2 or 3.3 at the most. Some guys get demerits and they get 3.8s and 3.9s."*

He says, "What do you do for your country?"

I said, "I play bridge and read the Cosmo."

He says, "There's your answer."

Q: What were you supposed to be doing?

Admiral Walker: Athletics, of course—being real athletic for good old Navy. But I was not an athlete, never have been. The only athletics I play now, I play golf now twice a week if I can possibly get it in. And I'm a horrible golfer, but I thoroughly enjoy being out with the boys. I never would be an athlete if I lived to be 900.

Q: Were you in any other extracurricular activities?

Admiral Walker: No. No, I wasn't in theater groups or anything like that.

---

*Lieutenant Commander Willard E. Cheadle, USN.

Walker #1 - 39

Q: Were there any midshipmen that you remember from the classes just ahead of you? For example, Arleigh Burke was two ahead of you.

Admiral Walker: Yes. I never knew Arleigh Burke as a midshipman at all.* No. I never knew the famous guy there, Rickover. He wasn't in my battalion. I never knew who he was. I don't think anybody at the Naval Academy knew who he was unless they roomed right near him. He was a nonentity. Hell, he didn't even stand as well at the Naval Academy as I did.**

Q: What did midshipmen do for spending money? It must have cost something over there in Paris and London.

Admiral Walker: Well, each cruise, my family gave me $100, which was a lot of money. Also the Navy gave us spending money in each port--not much, $15.00 or $20.00, as I remember. As a plebe, I got a monthly allowance of a dollar and a half. You'd go down to the midshipmen's store and buy a few pieces of candy and some cigarettes, that's about all. It kept you in cigarettes and a piece of candy once in a while. As a youngster, I got $3.00 a month, and as a second classman I got $8.00 a month, and as a

---
*Midshipman Arleigh A. Burke, USN, class of 1923. He later served as Chief of Naval Operations from 1955 to 1961.
**Midshipman Hyman G. Rickover, USN, class of 1922. Rickover stood 107th in his class of 539 graduates.

first classman I got $12.00 a month. Well, in general, I used to like to dance. I dragged to every dance I was eligible to go to from the time I became eligible. But it wasn't too expensive. It only cost you a dollar and a half, $3.00 for the two of you for dinner and a tip. Dinner was standard in all the restaurants in Annapolis at that time at a dollar and a half, and so if the girls came down, they paid their own hotel bill or drag house bill, wherever they happened to stay. Of course, you had to walk everywhere. I never was in an automobile the whole time I was a midshipman until I was a first classman in June Week. Not 'til June Week. Because you weren't permitted in an automobile, except when you were away from Annapolis on leave.

Q: Your parents must have become prosperous. You said they weren't too well off before.

Admiral Walker: Well, they weren't. I don't know how they ever got the hundred bucks together, but they did. Every year they gave me a hundred bucks to go on a cruise. But they never gave me anything at all during the year. As a matter of fact, the Superintendent used to write to all the parents and request them not to send any money to their midshipmen sons during the course of the academic year, because he said, "They have all they need to look after their proper needs." And that was it.

Walker #1 - 41

Q: What do you remember about the movie that was made at the Naval Academy during that period?

Admiral Walker: I don't remember too much about it except I was in a mob scene once or twice. That's about all I remember. I remember seeing Ramon Novarro. That's it.

Q: What do you recall of the graduation exercise?

Admiral Walker: I remember going up and getting my diploma and throwing my hat in the air. And I remember the anchor man in my class getting the anchor, but in those days, they didn't give the anchor man a dollar.* That's something that came in long after my time. All the anchor man got was an anchor to hang up in his room later on. They do pretty well now with a dollar apiece and 1,100 midshipmen graduating.

Q: Were you deliberately trying to stand as high in the class as you could?

Admiral Walker: In general, I wanted to be very sure that I didn't ever have to take any re-examinations. I always wanted to

---

*The anchor man is the one with the lowest cumulative standing in the class at the time of graduation. Current practice is that the anchor man receives a dollar from each of his classmates.

stand as well as I could, because we all realized that where we stood was our place in the Navy for the next 25 or 30 years. That's the way it was in those days. There was no deep down selection for promotion at all in those days. So we all knew that it paid to stand high. The officers, the instructors used to tell us that, too: "Don't forget, this is where you're going to be for life." Now, when we graduated, we got our ships by means of a raffle, and you selected a number, pulled it out. My number was a hundred and something. I hoped to become engaged to Miriam, who lived in Boston, so I was after a Boston battleship, which at that time, of course, was the Utah and the Florida. But by the time they got down to my number, all the openings in the Boston battleships were gone, so I selected the New York in Norfolk, and then I went around to see what I could do to talk one of my classmates that had no special reason for going to Boston into going to Norfolk and giving his option to me. And I finally talked one of my classmates by the name of Rollo Vanasse to go to Norfolk while I went to Boston to catch the USS Utah.*

Q: Was Prohibition observed at the Naval Academy?

Admiral Walker: Yes, it was. Definitely. And a few, very, very few used to get a drink. I never had a drink the whole time I

---

*Ensign Roland B. Vanasse, USN.

was at the Naval Academy, except on midshipman cruise. And my first drink I ever had in my life was at a bar in Panama, on my first midshipman youngster cruise. It was the first drink I ever had in my life, because I come from Maine, which had been dry since 1860. So it was nothing strange to me that there were no drinks around.

Q: Were there any regulations against smoking in Annapolis?

Admiral Walker: Yes. There had been regulations against smoking until Wilson came.* Wilson came at the same time I did, and about my plebe summer, I think, he put in the rule that we could smoke, but we could not smoke before breakfast. So everybody used to try to smoke before breakfast. And what they'd do, they'd try to get what they called a tendency, run the water in the shower and then hope that the air going out would draw the smoke out through the vent in the shower.** Just like kids. Just because they were prohibited, that's when everybody wanted to smoke, before breakfast.

Q: Where had you met your future wife?

Admiral Walker: I met her on my youngster September leave. I

---
*Rear Admiral Henry B. Wilson, USN, who was Superintendent during much of the time Walker was a midshipman.
**"Tendency" was a term for a draft of air.

went home, and she was visiting my girlfriend in Portland. And we went out for a Sunday afternoon walk, and that's all I saw of her until my leave was about over. Then I decided that maybe it might be a good idea to shift horses, so I wrote her in Boston and asked if I could stop by on my way back to the Naval Academy. She said yes, and I did, and stayed one day, I think it was. Then I didn't see her again until my second class September leave, when she came through Portland from Chebeague Island and I spent the afternoon with her at the movies. I didn't see her again until first class September leave, when I stopped off at her house in Newton Highlands, Massachusetts, and stayed four or five days. And then I didn't see her again until my June Week at the Naval Academy, when we became engaged.

Q: I guess the original girlfriend didn't like this arrangement too well.

Admiral Walker: I don't know what she thought. She never told me.

Q: Did they have a rule then that you had to wait for a while before you could get married?

Admiral Walker: No. I was married in October of '27.

Walker #1 - 45

Q: I think there were probably some who did not wait that long.

Admiral Walker: Some of my classmates were married on graduation day, so it was just after that, about the time of the Depression that they put in that two-year rule. No. Anybody in my class could get married right off. I know one who did, Bruce Kelley.* He was married on graduation day.

Q: But you didn't know her well enough then to get married?

Admiral Walker: No. I had just barely been engaged to her at June Week. I thought I did pretty well then. I had only seen her about a week in my whole life. But I had been writing to her for three full years.

Q: Describe the scene in the _Utah_ when you reported aboard then for duty.

Admiral Walker: Well, you see, we got up to Boston. We reported to the commandant of the Boston Navy Yard, but the _Utah_ was away on a midshipmen's cruise. So they sent all of us new ensigns to the Massachusetts Institute of Technology for the summer, for six weeks or so, for a course in gasoline engines, which was taught by a Dr. Fales, who was the head of the gasoline engine

---
*Ensign Bruce D. Kelley, USN.

Walker #1 - 46

department of MIT at that time.* So I don't have any recollection of us all trooping aboard the Utah when she came back from the cruise. I have no recollection of that at all.

Q: Was this course you took a useful one?

Admiral Walker: Yes. I've known how to fix my automobile all my life because of that. Up 'til now. I wouldn't touch one nowadays. Too many gadgets on one now.

Q: It probably had some carryover to the diesels then as you got into submarines.

Admiral Walker: That's right. And I remember one of the big exhibits he had there was a gasoline engine taken from the barge of a German admiral. There were very few diesels then. I can remember when we were in Goteborg, Sweden, of going into that exposition they had. They had one room where they had a big Swedish diesel engine for merchant ships set up.

Q: Did you enjoy the change in status now that you could report aboard ship as a commissioned officer?

---

*Dr. Dean A. Fales, who was on the faculty at MIT from 1916 to 1956.

Walker #1 - 47

Admiral Walker: Yes, definitely.

Q: How much difference did it make?

Admiral Walker: Well, I was fortunate enough that I was senior enough that I could get a room. There weren't rooms enough for all of us. We had about 25 or 30 of us reporting aboard. And they had taken the admiral's cabin and turned it into a bunk room, and all those that couldn't get a room were assigned to this bunk room, but I was senior enough so I was in a room with a mustang officer. No, I guess that was on the Florida. I can't recall for sure. But it was either the Florida or Utah I roomed with this mustang who had just fleeted up not too long ago from an enlisted man to an officer.

Q: You had been in the New York previously. How would you compare the ships in terms of how modern each class was?

Admiral Walker: Of course, the Utah and Florida were sister ships. The New York was two classes more modern. The first two all-big-gun ships were the Delaware and North Dakota. Then came the Florida and the Utah. Then came the Wyoming and Arkansas. And then came the New York and Texas. They were commissioned in 1914, the New York and Texas. And then after that came the Oklahoma, Nevada, and that class. I used to be able to name them

Walker #1 - 48

all and dates. I'm a little sketchy now.

Q: Did the New York have more amenities as far as living conditions?

Admiral Walker: Yes. She was quite comfortable except for all the bedbugs.

Q: When they converted the admiral's cabin into a bunk room, was the idea that these ships were so old they wouldn't have an admiral on board?

Admiral Walker: Yes. There was no idea that there would ever be an admiral on board, either on board the Utah or the Florida. We had a bunk room on both those ships. In the Florida, we didn't have too many from my class, but we had all the influx from '26. And when we went to the Utah, there was quite a few leftover ensigns from '24 on board to add to the ones from '25.

Q: Describe the relationship between you, as a junior officer, and some of the senior petty officers you encountered. Usually the senior petty officers take the ensigns in hand and train them.

Admiral Walker: I don't recall anything like that. I don't

recall any problems at all with the senior petty officers. In the *Utah*, I was in the deck division. I was in the second division, and I was the junior officer of the second division, and also the junior turret officer, which meant I was down below breaking out the shells and the powder to be sent up to the turret. And we didn't have a chief turret captain; we had a first class turret captain, and he was very good and helpful in teaching me a lot of things. I don't recall ever having any problem. We had a good chief boatswain's mate who taught me a lot of tricks. I remember an old enlisted man by the name of Caves. He'd been a chief about three times and busted each time, because he got drunk and disorderly. He'd been busted the last time down to seaman second class. But he was an older man; he looked funny in a sailor suit, compared with all the rest of them.

Q: I'll bet he did.

Admiral Walker: We didn't have any disciplinary problems in those days, practically none. The only time we had any problems, say, like we'd go into Gonaives, Haiti, some time and all the sailors would go ashore and get drunk. I can remember having shore duty one Sunday afternoon in Gonaives, and about 300 screaming, yelling drunk sailors all hitting the end of the dock at the same time. And it was just the grace of God we didn't get pushed off the end. Of course, we didn't have any drug problems in those days at all, and we had very little problem with alcohol. Of course, it was still Prohibition. We used to load up when we were in Guantanamo Bay, Cuba. I can remember one night helping to pull aboard 300 gallons of rum and about 200 quarts of various whiskeys and liqueurs. Peppy was the guy who ran the liquor. He loaded his boat and brought it out under the bow at night when we knew we had a sympathetic lieutenant on watch. We'd open up the porthole, put down a line with a hook and draw them up one at a time and then divide them up amongst us. Then you'd take the sheathing off the side of the ship, and put your liquor and so forth in there, put the sheathing back on, and screw it in, touch it up with paint, and you were all set until you got back to the States. I can remember the story--I don't know whether this is apocryphal or not, but a lot of people told me that the New York came into Norfolk either my first or second year as an ensign, and the exec said, "We're going to have an inspection tomorrow.* The boats will run all night tonight. I don't want any liquor found on this ship tomorrow." Those were some days.

Q: But you managed to get away with it in your ship, I take it.

Admiral Walker: Yes. Well, we'd take it ashore a little at a

---

*Exec--executive officer.

time. Normally, officers' baggage isn't inspected, so we'd take a bag ashore, we maybe have a couple of quarts in there or even a gallon of rum. We'd get it all off that way. We didn't try to unload it at once, oh, no. And each individual would take it off as it suited his convenience.

Q: Do you recall the captain or exec or any of the department heads from the Utah?

Admiral Walker: The captain was Captain Sexton. He later became Rear Admiral Sexton.* I remember he put me under hack for one day.** When we were in the navy yard, the division officer was on leave. I was supposed to report the division quarters in the morning, at 9:00 o'clock. Well, I overslept and I didn't get up there, so the next thing I knew, the exec wanted to see me, and then the skipper wanted to see me. The skipper put me under hack for one day, because I didn't get up to quarters. That was the only disciplinary action I ever had in the Navy.

Q: Was there any disgrace in that?

Admiral Walker: No, not so much. It happened all the time to people, to some more than others, especially in the smaller

---
*Captain Walton R. Sexton, USN.
**"Hack" is a colloquial term for punishment of officers by confining them to their quarters for a specified period of time.

ships. Some of these younger lieutenant commanders and so forth, were apt to be a little freer with putting their junior officers under hack. But, fortunately, I never did. In fact, my years as a junior officer in the Boston battleships just were very happy and instructive. And when the time came that I knew I was going to be transferred, I asked for torpedo school, because that was a six-month course. And then I had in mind that I'd try to get a request to go from torpedo school to submarine school, which would give me a whole year's shore duty when I was first married. Well, all of a sudden one day I was called up and told that I had just been designated to volunteer for submarine school. So I went to submarine school in June 1927, and I was married on October 8, '27. They let me off from submarine school about noon on Friday, in time for me to get to Newton Highlands, Massachusetts, for the wedding rehearsal Friday night. On Saturday night, we spent our wedding night in the Ritz Carlton in Boston. We had dinner Sunday with Mrs. Walker's family and drove to New London that evening with all our possessions so that I could be in school on Monday morning. The drive to New London was made in a driving rainstorm.

I graduated submarine school--I think it was the day that the S-4 was sunk off Provincetown.* So when I got home back to Boston that day with my new wife, her family wasn't too pleased

---

*On 17 December 1927, the USS S-4 (SS-109) sank after being rammed by the Coast Guard cutter Paulding off Provincetown, Cape Cod, Massachusetts.

Walker #1 - 53

with the idea that she was married to a submarine officer.

Q: What were your views on the subject? You say you were volunteered to do this. Did you object?

Admiral Walker: No, you didn't in those days. The exec just called me in and said the ship had to supply 10-12 officers to submarine school: "You've been designated to volunteer to go to submarine school." That was all there was. A few days later, my orders came through and I was in submarines. I was in submarines off and on for 15 years.

Q: But was it something you wanted to do, though?

Admiral Walker: Yes, but I wanted to get, if I could, torpedo school in between so as to get myself a year's shore duty.

Q: Why did you wind up being on two battleships there in Boston, both the Utah and the Florida?

Admiral Walker: Well, I don't know. In general, as I say, they'd send about 25 of the junior officers to one of the East Coast battleships. Then, at the end of the first year, approximately half or more were ordered off to small ships like destroyers, some to torpedo school, but I wasn't ordered. I was

Walker #1 - 54

just ordered, with 10 or 12 ensigns, to the Florida rather than being ordered to a small ship or one of the train, or what have you.*

Q: Do you have any specific recollections of the Florida as opposed to the Utah?

Admiral Walker: Oh, the only thing I remember, she was an oil-burner. We didn't have to coal ship anymore. That was a big remembrance of the Florida. Otherwise, she was a carbon copy of the Utah. On the Florida, I was in the engineering department, and I remember I was qualified for top watch in the engineering department at that time, and I was also on watch when we made our trial runs off Rockland, speed runs, to see what the ship would do after she had been reboilered and so forth.**

Q: This was after she was converted from coal to oil?

Admiral Walker: This was after she was converted. See, she got the battle cruiser boilers--the battle cruisers from World War I that weren't built--were given to the Florida and the Utah,

---
*The logistic support ships of that period were known collectively as the fleet train.
**The Navy frequently tested new or converted ships on a measured mile run off the coast of Rockland, Maine.

because the Utah was modernized a year later.* The Florida had had 12 B&W coal-burning boilers and she ended up with four of these battle cruiser boilers. And we went up to Rockland for trials, and we made 22.36 knots, which made us the fastest battleship in the Navy at that time.

Q: Well, they planned for those battle cruisers to be fast, so that made sense. Were you there during the yard period when she was converted?

Admiral Walker: No, that was the year I was in the Utah. The Florida was being converted all that year while I was in the Utah. Then, the year I went to the Florida, the Utah was being converted. When I finished the Florida, also the Utah was finished. They were both running. Of course, then I went to submarine school when I left the Florida.

Q: Well, that's a pretty substantial operation, putting new boilers in a ship, isn't it?

Admiral Walker: Oh, yes, it sure is, especially when you're taking out 12 and putting in four and shifting from coal to oil.

---

*A number of planned U.S. battle cruisers were not built because of the Washington naval disarmament agreements of 1921-1922. The first two ships of the class, Lexington and Saratoga, were converted from battle cruisers to aircraft carriers while under construction.

You've got to change all those coal bunkers to oil bunkers. Of course, the main engine part of it remains the same; there was no change there. And the evaporators and all that part, the auxiliaries, remained the same. But you had to put air locks in the boiler rooms, because the boilers were run under air pressure in the boiler room. In coal-burning, you had open firerooms. You did have some blowers that you could blow in some air to help speed up combustion when you wanted to speed up with the coal, but it wasn't a closed fireroom like you had in oil-burning ships.

Q: Did they have the reciprocating engines?

Admiral Walker: No, they both had turbines. My only duty in a reciprocating engine ship was in the New York. The New York had reciprocating engines, even though she was built six years later. Both the New York and Texas had reciprocating engines.

Q: One after that, the Oklahoma, had reciprocating engines.

Admiral Walker: I never had anything to do with the West Coast ships. I never had a day's duty on the West Coast. I had three tours of duty in Hawaii, but never had a day's duty on the West Coast.

Walker #1 - 57

Q: That's amazing.

Admiral Walker: Isn't it?

Q: What do you recall about those engineering watches? What kinds of things were you, as the top watch stander, concerned with?

Admiral Walker: I was concerned with the condition of the main engines, if they were properly lubricated, that all the pressures and so forth in the various components were all in the proper place, proper readings. And see to it that the throttle men all answered the bells from the bridge correctly, the evaporators were working okay, we were getting plenty of fresh water for the boilers, and that the water was good. If the water wasn't good enough for the boilers, they put it in the ship's tanks for drinking.

Q: Boilers deserved better than people.

Admiral Walker: That is right, because the trouble was, once in a while you'd get it contaminated with a little salt. Salt is not good for the boilers. It didn't hurt the people a bit. It was good. It gave more taste to the straight distilled water, so we didn't mind that. But it almost sounds funny--if the water wasn't good enough for the boilers, you give it to the people to drink.

Q: What was the overall caliber of the enlisted people then?

Admiral Walker: It was very good. It was fine. They weren't as well educated as they became later on, but they were good, conscientious, hard-working kids.

There is an anecdote on the <u>Florida</u>. We had for our exec "Ditty Box" Mayo, quite a character in the Navy, who had been in charge of all the Navy athletes going to the 1920 Olympics, and had gone to his head, I think.[*] He was a great character. I remember they used to have what they called mess nights once in a while. Well, the first mess night, we all had to come in our full evening dress and bring our girls. Well, that was fine. Everybody came. The second night, only about half the ensigns came. He called us all up and wanted to know why we hadn't shown up. And Red Harlow--he was the first man to talk--he said, "Well, Commander, I didn't have a clean, white vest. It was dirty and I hadn't got it back."[**]

He said, "Every man should have at least three waistcoats."

Q: So Mayo was kind of tough?

---

[*]Commander Claude B. Mayo, USN, executive officer.
[**]Ensign James B. Harlow, USN.

Walker #1 - 59

Admiral Walker: Yes, he was tough. He was a character.

Q: Who was the skipper of the <u>Florida</u>?

Admiral Walker: David F. Boyd. Captain Boyd was very nice and a good seaman. He had a young son, about eight or nine, who upset some of the officers in the wardroom by his table manners.

Q: Was Mayo interested in athletics on board ship since he'd been to the Olympics?

Admiral Walker: Yes. I'll tell you about it. We were always having smokers and that sort of thing. We had this very good light heavyweight boxer by the name of Ernie Schaaf, and Ernie fought in semi-professional boxing, and he did very well. All the crew of the <u>Florida</u>, whenever he would fight, right around Boston, they used to all go to the matches, and every once in a while, he'd be fighting a black boy. And every time that he'd knock him out, they'd all sing, "Bye, Bye, Blackbird." It got to be famous around Boston, the <u>Florida</u>'s crew singing "Bye, Bye, Blackbird." And then when he got out of the Navy, he went into professional boxing, and he was killed as a professional boxer in a fight, three or four years after he got out of the Navy.* But he was a nice young kid, very sharp.

Q: Were you then dating your future wife a good bit during this period?

Admiral Walker: Oh, yes. Whenever I was in Boston, I practically lived at her house.

Q: What was the operating pattern for the battleships during that time?

Admiral Walker: We'd go down to Cuba some time in the latter part of September, and we'd be in Cuba until just before Christmas. We'd come back for the Christmas holidays. Then we'd go down to Guantanamo from January until May, and we'd run all our exercises from Guantanamo. We generally had a small exercise with the rest of the Atlantic fleet, and one year we had a combined exercise with the Pacific Fleet, because they came east through the canal, and we had a combined exercise with them.

---

*After a short hitch in the Navy, Schaaf pursued a career as a boxer, first as an amateur, then a professional. Fighting a heavyweight match against Primo Carnera at Madison Square Garden on 10 February 1933, Schaaf was knocked out in the 13th round by what appeared a routine punch to the face. Schaaf was operated on but died on 14 February; he was 25 years old at his death. It was later determined that he went into the fight with a brain inflammation which diminished his ability to defend himself and made him unusually susceptible to brain damage.

Walker #1 - 61

Now, when I was in the _Florida_, the last night before we got into Boston, the last trip coming back from Cuba in the spring of 1927, I was on watch from 4:00 to 8:00 in the morning, and I got word that my father had died, a dispatch that my father had died. So I went home for the funeral. I remember that very well.

Q: How much interest and awareness was there in the fleet then on naval aviation?

Admiral Walker: Not too much. The ships didn't carry any planes in those days, back in the middle Twenties. I don't think we even had the first carrier then.

Q: The _Langley_ came out around '22 or '23.*

Admiral Walker: Maybe the _Langley_ was down there. I can't recall for sure. I think maybe she was, the _Langley_, yes. But there wasn't too much awareness. Of course, it was sometime around that time that they had the Billy Mitchell bombings down there off the Virginia Capes somewhere, but people didn't think too much of those tests.** They said, "Hell, the damn ship is

---
*The Navy's first aircraft carrier, the USS _Langley_ (CV-1) was commissioned 20 March 1922.
 **Brigadier General William Mitchell, U.S. Army, conducted tests against obsolete battleships in the early 1920s to demonstrate his thesis that the capability for aerial bombing supposedly made surface warships vulnerable and therefore useless in wartime.

stopped. No wonder. A child could hit it with it stopped." Under way--that's something else again.

Q: Were submarines considered a more desirable thing to go into then than aviation?

Admiral Walker: No, I don't think so. Most of the submariners in my day went into submarines the same way I did. They were designated volunteers.

Q: The difference then was that it wasn't as permanent, I guess, as it later became.

Admiral Walker: That is right.

Q: You moved in and out.

Admiral Walker: That's right, a lot of them did. A lot of them took only one tour in submarines. I was in from '27 to '42--15 years. Of course, I wasn't at sea all that time.

Q: Well, for example, you had a destroyer command later. That wouldn't happen today.

Admiral Walker: Oh, no. See, when I stepped aboard that

destroyer as commanding officer, that was my first day's duty in a destroyer. I was the skipper. Of course, I had had command before. Command is command. The ship may handle a little bit differently, although it was a bad thing in one way because I had no conception of surface tactics. An officer who grows up in destroyers and the battleships really has had a lot of experience before he gets a chance at command. He's had a lot of experience with surface tactics. I had none.

Q: Had you gotten on the bridge at all when you were on the battleships?

Admiral Walker: My first year, when I was on the deck duty, I was junior officer of the deck.

Q: But surface action in 1926 was a good deal different than '42.

Admiral Walker: Yes. And the junior officer of the deck didn't have too much to do. He had to see to it that the lookouts kept alert, do anything that the officer of the deck asked him to do, write up the log for the officer of the deck, watch to see that the helmsmen and the engine telegraphs were operating properly and the ship stayed on course.

Q: Did you get any involvement in formation steaming and maneuvering the battleships?

Admiral Walker: Practically none. We'd get a little each year we were down at Guantanamo, and I can remember having the exec call us all on the bridge when we were in heavy maneuvers so we could watch it and see what was going on. By the way, my first exec was a very famous guy. He was killed on the bridge of the Arizona at Pearl Harbor. He was the admiral, I.C. Kidd.*

Q: What do you recall of Kidd from the Utah?

Admiral Walker: He was a wonderful exec. All the ensigns loved him. When we were in Guantanamo, he used to organize swimming parties. We would take the ship's motorboat, and we'd all go over to a little inlet there at the officers' club and go swimming every morning at 6:00 o'clock. I didn't like the 6:00 o'clock so much, but it seemed to be the thing to do. I never did go for early rising.

Q: I'm with you on that.

Was there a lot of on-the-job training in the battleships for you as an officer?

---

*Rear Admiral Isaac C. Kidd, USN, Commander Battleship Division One was killed in the attack on his flagship on 7 December 1941.

Walker #1 - 65

Admiral Walker: Yes. And also we were all supposed to keep journals, which we used to have to turn in. I sometimes think that what I used to turn in was pretty sad.

Q: Why? Weren't you too diligent about it?

Admiral Walker: I wasn't diligent about it; I wasn't too good a writer anyway. Pretty sad.

Q: What do you recall of submarine school?

Admiral Walker: I'll never forget my first dive in submarines. We had the O-boats, for school boats, and I was assigned to the pump room aft of the main engine room. In those boats, you blew some of the water out of the main ballast tanks with high-pressure air. When the boat came to the surface, a low-pressure pump took over and pumped all the water out of the ballast tanks. Those boats were small, and you were awfully confined there, and I'm a big guy, and I remember that, my very first time, I was way back there in the pump room of the old O-something. I don't know which one it was, but it was an O-boat. We had four school boats: O-1, O-2, O-3, and O-4.

Q: Did you get claustrophobia at all?

Admiral Walker: No, never did. I can still remember two of the characters in our class, names were Dutch Will and Mickey O'Regan in '23.*

Q: Dutch Will later became an admiral.

Admiral Walker: He later became an admiral and head of American Export Lines. And Dutch Will was also with me on the staff just before the war started. He was engineer officer of the staff. I can remember a story on Dutch. We went inspecting one of the tenders. Dutch made a comment on our report that the tender couldn't be doing a very good job because its machine shop was so clean. Oh, boy! Did the commander in chief blow up on that one, because in the Navy, you know, cleanliness is next to godliness, and to have this young whippersnapper lieutenant commander saying that the ship couldn't be doing a very good job because its machine shop was so clean--that really caused a commotion.

Q: What period was this when that happened?

Admiral Walker: This is when I was on the staff. This would be in the summer of 1941, just before the war.

---

*Lieutenant (junior grade) John M. Will, USN; Lieutenant (junior grade) William V. O'Regan, USN.

Walker #1 - 67

Q: And so the commander in chief would be Admiral Kimmel?*

Admiral Walker: That's correct. That's correct. I'll never forget that blowup.

Q: How much preparation and training did you have ashore before you went out in the submarines for the first time?

Admiral Walker: We had classroom training every day from about 9:00 until 4:00, or maybe once or twice a week we'd spend up to half a day out on the submarines making dives and learning how to make approaches and that sort of thing and learning how to handle all the gear, the diving planes and so forth.

Q: Did you find that you liked this kind of a new existence?

Admiral Walker: Yes, I liked it. I liked it. And the big thing, of course, I liked about it was that you got more responsibility very young than you get any other place in the Navy. When I graduated from submarine school, I was given a month's leave and ordered to the R-8 in Pearl Harbor.

Q: Got more pay, too?

---
*Admiral Husband E. Kimmel, USN, Commander in Chief Pacific Fleet. Will and Walker were then on the staff of Commander Submarines Scouting Force.

Admiral Walker: No.

Q: Really?

Admiral Walker: No, in those days there was no extra pay for officers. Sailors got $1.00 a dive up to 15 dives per month, and the dives had to be for at least an hour. If you didn't make 15 dives, they lost money. So what we'd do, we'd get toward the end of the month, when I was out at Pearl Harbor where I was attached after submarine school, if we didn't have the 15 dives, we'd back out from the pier, sit on the bottom of the bay there until we had an hour, then come back up again and go to the pier, because that's what we did to get 15 bucks for our sailors. No, I never got an extra dime all the time I was in submarines until World War II. When the war started, or just before that, I was operations officer for Commander Submarines Pacific Fleet. And I'd get orders to go down and visit submarines every day. I'd go down and have coffee with the skipper and he'd sign my orders, and I'd get my extra 25%.

Q: Did you seem to have a knack for handling the boats when you got out into them?

Admiral Walker: I never had any problems as a shiphandler. If I say so myself, I think I was a good shiphandler.

Q: Do you think that was something innate, or did you practice a lot at it?

Admiral Walker: Observing, mostly. Nobody ever really taught you anything. You observed and asked questions—that's the way you learned to be a shiphandler. I think they teach it nowadays, but in my day, they didn't teach you anything. You were just supposed to learn it.

Q: Then when you're ready, you can take over.

Admiral Walker: Yes.

Q: Are there any of the instructors from the submarine school that you particularly remember?

Admiral Walker: Yeah, the one I remember the most was Carroll Bonney.* He was in '20. He had given us a classroom exercise on the dangers of explosions from storage batteries, and he hooked up this small glass storage battery and shot the juice to it from a generator. And the next thing we were all watching and the damn thing blew up in our faces. The skipper of the submarine school at that time was Ernie J. King.**

---

*Lieutenant Carroll T. Bonney, USN.
**Captain Ernest J. King, USN, later Chief of Naval Operations and Commander in Chief U.S. Fleet during World War II.

Walker #1 - 70

Q: Did you have much contact with him?

Admiral Walker: No, no. He was commanding officer of the submarine base in New London, and there was a separate commanding officer of the submarine school who was a commander. I forget now who that was.

Q: There had been the S-4 tragedy and the S-51.

Admiral Walker: Well, there had been the S-51 tragedy, but the S-4 tragedy didn't occur until the day I graduated from submarine school. Now the S-51 occurred before I went to submarine school, as I recall it.* That was off Block Island. A strange thing. My second commanding officer in the R-8 was George Dana, in '20, and he had been attached to the S-51 and detached just two or three days before it was sunk.**

Q: I'm wondering if there was any thought given to how people would be rescued or try to escape from those submarines at that time.

Admiral Walker: It wasn't until I got out to Pearl that

---

*On the night of 25 September 1925, the USS S-51 (SS-162) was rammed and sunk by the merchant steamer City of Rome. Only three survivors were recovered from the 36 men in the submarine.
**Lieutenant George M. Dana, USN, who commanded the USS R-8 (SS-85) when Walker was serving on board in 1931.

provision was made for escape. Then they put in skirts on the hatches. These skirts you could let down so you could flood the compartment and it would go up so far and hit the skirt and then wouldn't rise anymore because there was a big air bubble up there. Then you could duck down under the skirt and come up. That was about the time also they were developing the Momsen lung.* We had Momsen lungs. As I remember the Momsen lung, you were supposed to pump it up first with oxygen. You had outlets from oxygen bottles right there at the escape hatches. Also, they changed the form of the escape hatch so there was a flat surface around the skirt so that the diving bell would sit down on it, so you could come up and get in the diving bell and get out. Also, they put in a hatch that you could open from either the outside or the inside with a wheel. When I first went in the R-8, to close the hatch, you had a bar that went across and a crank. So unless there was somebody inside to open it, you couldn't get in. No way. No way.

Going to my first duty from submarine school, January 1928, in Honolulu, you had to be very careful, because you only made one mistake. As soon as you crossed the bar out of Pearl Harbor and went out 300 or 400 yards, you were in 2,000 fathoms of water. So you made one mistake and that was your last one. So you had to be careful.

---
*The Momsen lung was a rescue breathing device developed by submariner Charles B. Momsen. It gave submariners a source of oxygen to breathe while ascending from a disabled submarine.

Q: Was the escape tower in New London at that point?

Admiral Walker: No. It was when I came back. I came back to New London for a year's duty in the R-13 from '31 to '32, and the escape tower was there then, and we all had to take a training session and learn how to use the Momsen lung.

Q: During that period in the Twenties when you were still in the submarine school, was there any real hope for somebody trapped underwater in a submarine?

Admiral Walker: Not really. Now, even the S-boats at that time, like the S-4, I don't think there was any way. I think she had the same sort of hatch arrangements that we had in the R-8—just a bar across it, fitted into indentations in the hull, and you cranked it up tight against that. No, it was some time while I was out in Pearl that they put in those new hatches. I don't remember just when it was.

Q: How much time did you spend on board a submarine as compared to living in a tender or what have you? How were the living accommodations?

Admiral Walker: Well, in the R-boats, we had one built-in bunk for the skipper and a couple of pipe frame bunks just forward of

Walker #1 - 73

that hanging on the bulkhead for the second and third officers. There were only three officers. We had three officers and a complement of 25 men. Right in this officer part, there was a little table like a card table and three chairs around it, and that's where we ate. Nobody had a separate room at all.

Q: How long would you go to sea at a given time?

Admiral Walker: The longest normally we ever went was for 14 days. What did they call those? We had a 14-day sort of war patrol, simulated war patrol cruises. Once a year we had to do that. Once every six years, we had to make a 200-foot dive.

Q: Where did you go on these war patrols?

Admiral Walker: To Lahaina Roads.* Normally that's where we went.

Q: Where did you spend the time in between times, when you weren't out at sea?

Admiral Walker: Well, we had a big office on shore. We had 20 R-boats out there at that time. The R-1 to R-10 was the Ninth

---

*Lahaina Roads, off the island of Maui, was a frequent U.S. Fleet operating area during the 1930s.

Division, and the R-11 to R-20 was the 14th Division. And then we had a squadron commander, two division commanders. Each division had a division commander and the squadron had a squadron commander. And we had a big office. On one side there was a row of ten desks, room for two people at a desk and somebody else in chairs, enough for everybody. And on the other side of this long room were the desks and so forth of the other division. And at the end of the room on one side was the division commander's office. On the other side was the other division commander's office. The squadron commander--I forget now where his office used to be. I think we had the USS Chicago then as a station ship, and when we had to stay out there overnight on duty, as I recall it, we slept in the Chicago.* And then when they built the new Chicago, they changed its name to the Alton.

Q: She was one of the first steel cruisers.

Admiral Walker: She was one of the first steel cruisers, right. She was painted white then. I don't think she could move. She was anchored to a pier at that time.

Q: These offices you were in, were these in the same place the submarine base has been in later years?

---

*The old cruiser Chicago (CL-14) served as a tender at Pearl Harbor from 1919 until decommissioned in 1923. She was then a barracks ship until 1935; she was renamed Alton on 16 July 1928 and reclassified IX-5.

Admiral Walker: That's right, the same place. The first tour, I don't remember that we had a diving tank there. When I came back the second time, in command of the S-21, there was a tank there, much like they had at New London.

Q: Sounds as if they were built about the same time.

Admiral Walker: Yes, I think they were. I don't know exactly, but it was somewhere between 1930 and 1935, because I took command of the S-21 in June of '35.

Q: Where did the enlisted men spend their time when the boat was in port?

Admiral Walker: They had barracks. They were screened, and the men all had bunks in this. There was also a mess hall for the men. When we'd go out for a day, we'd draw enough food for a noon meal. If we'd go out for, say, 14 days, we'd just have to get as much as we could. We didn't have any ice machines. We had literally an icebox. If there was enough ice in it for three days, you couldn't get any food in it. If there was food in it, you couldn't get any ice in it. So, in effect, we lived on cans. And it was somewhere around 1929 that they put in ice makers in each one of the iceboxes in the R-boats. We thought we had died and gone to heaven. First of all, we could keep a lot more

Walker #1 - 76

perishable food than we ever could before. And, of course, in a submarine, the officers and the crew all eat the same chow. It all came out of the same frying pan.

Q: So you did have some cooking faciliites.

Admiral Walker: All you had was like a grill top stove and an oven; that's all you had, and we had one mess boy to look after us. He was usually a Filipino boy, and he served our meals.

Q: I guess you'd need a vent to get rid of that frying smoke and so forth.

Admiral Walker: Of course, the diesels did that, because you'd generally run with the main hatch, the conning tower, open, and those diesels, of course, take an awful lot of air. And we didn't have snorkels or anything like that in those days. And that would just pull the air right through the boat. But so many days of this 14-day war patrol, you had to be submerged all day long. Well, I tell you, with 25 or 30 sweating people in that boat and with water that was 80-degree temperature, by the time you surfaced at night, things were pretty raunchy. It was really something. And then as a part of that cruise and training, we always had to fire a long-range battle practice, too. There we'd submerge and make attack on a target; then we'd come up and fire

16, 18 rounds from the 3-inch gun, make the gun waterproof again, because when you came up, you had to get off all the waterproof equipment, get the shells up through the hatch, load the gun and fire and then put all the waterproofing equipment on the gun, back down the hatch, back down to diving depth, and then fire water slugs out of the torpedo tubes. It was really quite a thing, and you only had a very short time. I forget now what the timing was, but it wasn't very much. You really had to train for it.

Q: I would think that the men would have to be pretty versatile if you had only 25 men to do all the jobs on board the submarine.

Admiral Walker: They did have to be. We'd generally have about eight or ten in the engineering department, and then you'd generally have a chief petty officer and two or three electricians. And you had a quartermaster and a signalman and about eight or ten seamen second class. I know we had one enlisted man by the name of Howley. He was a first class quartermaster. That kid could dive the boat all by himself. He could sound the diving alarm, go down the hatch, close the hatch, come down into the control room, grab the bow and stern planes—the stern planes with the left hand, the bow planes with the right hand, because they were electrically operated—and dive the boat all by himself. He was very good, and he was a kid that they picked off the New York waterfront just after World War I.

Q: Did he later get commissioned, do you know?

Admiral Walker: No, I don't think so. He was too old by the time the war came along. I know the exec and I had to get out and get downtown one night to keep him from marrying a leper. Oh, gee. Those enlisted men were just like children, you know, in those days.

Q: Did an officer have that kind of control over enlisted men's lives?

Admiral Walker: Yeah. Of course, it wasn't written down in the regulation book, but we had it. We had complete control, no problem. Of course, we worked under "rocks and shoals," which is a lot different from the book today, which is a pain in the neck.* I wouldn't want to work under that. You had a lot of control in the "rocks and shoals," and everybody knew it. And, of course, you lived right on top of the enlisted men. You got a very liberal education about sex in a very short time. As somebody said, "If they weren't doing it, they were talking about it." Holy mackerel! As the sailors used to say, "If she's big

---

*"Rocks and shoals" was the standard nickname for Articles for the Government of the Navy, which was used until after World War II.

enough, she's old enough." Oh, they were something.

Q: Did the skippers stand underway watches?

Admiral Walker: They had to in the R-boats and O-boats, because there were only three of us. We usually stood one in three. In the S-boats, we had four officers. The skipper didn't stand watch. And I liked that. My only duty in an S-boat was when I was commanding officer, so I enjoyed that, and I had a separate room. That was really magnificent to have a separate room.

Q: I would gather you'd be pretty tired at the end of 14 days of that three-section watch.

Admiral Walker: Oh, you would be. We took one trip from Pearl Harbor to San Diego in the spring of 1930. It took us 15 days from Pearl Harbor to San Diego. For the first three days, we were in almost a typhoon, and every other wave was going right over the bridge, so you had to lash yourself to the bridge. And so much water was coming down the hatch that part of the time we could only run on one engine, because we couldn't get enough air through the high induction to run on two engines. And so after two days, we could still see the light on the north of Molokai. That was really something. That was quite a trip.

Walker #1 - 80

Q: What do you recall generally about the maintenance procedures in those boats in that era?

Admiral Walker: They were excellent. We had standard instructions like you'd get for your automobile. At the end of so much time you would check this, and at the end of so much time you check that and the other thing. And in general, the boats were very well kept up. We had those old NELSECO diesel engines, which were a pain in the neck, because you had air injection, and the air compressors were very tricky. The rings on the high-pressure piston would get worn out on them easily, and then you couldn't get pressure enough to force the diesel oil into the cylinders. Because you had, of course, more pressure behind the diesel oil than there was pressure in the cylinder. Of course, the diesel engine, she takes one stroke and draws in air, and then the next stroke, she comes up and compresses the air and compresses it enough so the heat goes high enough to ignite the fuel oil when it's sprayed into the cylinder. Then the compression comes down to drive her. Well, all the diesels now have fuel injection. In other words, the oil is squirted into the cylinders under pressure, rather than it being driven in by air pressure like they were in those old NELSECO diesels. That's

New London Ship and Engine Company diesels.*

Q: Were they pretty reliable engines?

Admiral Walker: Well, yes and no. I was engineer officer for about three and a half years. They could cause you lots of headaches. I remember one endurance run we were on, the air pressure, we couldn't get enough. We hooked up to the air compressors for compressing air to put in the air bottles, hook that into the system to see what we could get, and the engine room was just black with smoke. You couldn't see where you were going. We finally had to give up the run. We just couldn't get air enough to run the diesels.

Another time, we made a trip over to Kauai, and on the way back, one engine conked out and then another engine conked out, and we were anchored just around the corner from Barbers Point. We also had trouble with our radio, so we couldn't send any messages. First thing we know, out comes the boat looking for us to see what had happened to us.

Q: Fortunately, you hadn't gone too far.

---

*In the years before World War I, the Electric Boat Company, a U.S. submarine builder, formed a corporation known as New London Ship and Engine Company (NELSECO), through which it arranged a licensing agreement with the British Vickers firm and the German Maschinenfabrik-Augsberg-Nurnberg (MAN) to build submarine diesels.

Walker #1 - 82

Admiral Walker: No. But that was quite a little trip. I don't know, 50 or 60 miles from Oahu over to Nawiliwili and Kauai.*

Q: How reliable were communications in those days in submarines?

Admiral Walker: Pretty good. When I commanded the S-21, I had a first class radioman who used to amaze me. He'd sit down at night and copy the press and read a book at the same time.** I never could really become proficient as a radio operator. I knew the code, and if it came slow enough, I could do it, but this guy, he'd take press and read a book at the same time. Just amazing.

Q: Some of those guys were very proficient.

Admiral Walker: You wouldn't believe it, what these guys could do.

Q: You talked about these division and squadron commanders in this main office. Are there any names of those that you recall?

---

*Kauai is one of the islands in the Hawaiian chain, situated west northwest of Oahu. Nawiliwili is one of Kauai's principal anchorages.
**A source of news for submarines at sea was the broadcast of press reports in Morse Code.

Admiral Walker: My first skipper in the R-8 was Edward I. McQuiston of '21. He's dead now. My second skipper was George H. Dana, in '20. He's still alive. He was at the top of the age limit in his class; he must be pretty close to 90.* He's living down in Norfolk now. There was one skipper when I first went over there in the R-6 was R. R. Stogsdall, in '20.** All these names are just lurking in the back of my mind, and I can't pull them out. At one time I could name every skipper in that division without any problem. Our division commander was Red Doyle, class of '17.*** I can't think offhand. I just can't think.

Q: Did the boats operate together very much?

Admiral Walker: No. No. Practically all operations were single. Most of the time, we were like bankers. We were out at 8:00 o'clock in the morning and back and tied up at 4:00 o'clock in the afternoon. And we'd run target practice on either destroyers or these rescue vessels or something of that nature. Anything that was available was used for a target to fire torpedoes, then have to pick the torpedoes up and bring them in.

Q: So these people in the chain of command were administrative

---

*George H. Dana was born 19 December 1896.
**Lieutenant Ralph R. Stogsdall, Jr., USN, commanding officer, R-6.
***Lieutenant Commander Walter E. Doyle, USN, Commander Submarine Division Nine.

Walker #1 - 84

only, I take it.

Admiral Walker: That is correct. They were administrative only.

Q: Did you go through the competitive exercise cycle during that period?

Admiral Walker: Oh, yes. We all shot for competition, and we had battle efficiency inspections when we'd have the division commander on board. He'd run us through our paces and see how we handled things. I know one skipper's name was George Bauernschmidt. He later was in Supply Corps, an admiral, and he went color-blind.

Q: He lives near Annapolis.

Admiral Walker: Yes. This is a story—it may be apocryphal; I don't know.* Old Tommy Hart came out, commander of Submarines Scouting Force, or Commander Submarines, I guess he was, U.S. Fleet at that time. He came out to inspect us. He inspected the R-2 that Bauernschmidt had, so Bauernschmidt took him out. And

---

*This story probably is apocryphal. Lieutenant (junior grade) George W. Bauernschmidt, USN, commanded the R-2 in 1927 and 1928. Rear Admiral Thomas C. Hart, USN, did not take over as Commander Submarine Divisions Battle Fleet until mid-1929. The situation could have occurred with different individuals involved.

after he got out through the channel and ready to go to sea, the admiral said to him, he said, "Nice work, Captain. It's just like the coxswain of a motor sailer would have done it." Because we didn't take any bearings or anything else. We knew that channel by heart.

Q: We have his oral history, Bauernschmidt, and he went into the Supply Corps not because he wanted to but that was the only way he could stay in the Navy.

Admiral Walker: That's right. He went color-blind, yes. "Cupie" Graubart, a classmate of mine, he was in the R-2 with him. Harry Sanders in '23 was in the R-8 with me.* And then he was detached in June of '29, and Murray Tichenor came to the R-8, and he was in '24.** So I never got to be above the third officer of the R-8 for three and a half years.

Q: Well, I'm sure you learned a lot in that time.

Admiral Walker: I got the least desirable jobs all the time.

Q: Such as?

---
*Lieutenant (junior grade) Harry Sanders, USN.
**Lieutenant (junior grade) Murray J. Tichenor, USN.

Walker #1 - 86

Admiral Walker: Chief engineer and communicator; navigator I was part of the time, too. But we didn't do much navigation, because we were just running from one headland to another, in general, out there. Of course, we took that trip to San Diego, but I was busy with the engines. I think Murray was doing the navigating, but then we were taking sights and plotting our position. We had to report our position every day to the division commander.

Q: Who handled the supply function in those boats?

Admiral Walker: Nobody.

Q: You had to get your food and fuel.

Admiral Walker: The engineer saw to it he had the engineering parts he needed. The C&R officer saw to it that he had the construction and repair parts that he needed. And the commissary officer saw to it that he had the food that we needed. I had a little trouble with the food, because you couldn't lock up anything, and they'd eat it too fast. So what I did, I'd figure out how long we were going to be at sea and how much that was in money for food, and I had the chief commissary steward go up and buy that much food. Then I said to the crew, "Go ahead, eat all you want to. When it's gone, there ain't no more. That's it. You aren't going to run me in debt anymore." Because they used to raise hell if you spent more than your food allowance. So that's the way I fixed them.

Q: Did that work?

Admiral Walker: Oh, it worked beautifully. They didn't eat much 'til the last couple of days, most of them.

Q: Describe Hawaii as a place to live in that era.

Admiral Walker: Ah! Hawaii was the land of milk and honey in those days. The Royal Hawaiian had just been built; it was brand-new. The Moana was there, and the Halekulani, and that was it down on the beach. There was practically nothing on the far side of Kalakaua Avenue. The surfboard club was down there on the beach, down towards Diamond Head somewhere, and it was just a little wooden building. When we first got there, the skipper, Lieutenant E. I. McQuiston, took us in for two or three days, and then we found a little one-bedroom furnished house, very small, for $50 a month, and we lived in that for four or five months. And then we moved to a new development on the Ala Wai Canal, and we were one of the first people to live on the Ala Wai Canal. The only way you could get to Pearl Harbor was by your own car or by a train. But the trains ran so that they were no help to you. It's about 10 or 12 miles out to Pearl Harbor. So the only way you got back and forth was by automobile, and we lived in town the whole time. There were no quarters at all on the submarine base. There were some quarters in the navy yard for the navy yard people and also for a few of the doctors, but that's all. All the submariners all lived in town. Very few of the enlisted men were married; they couldn't afford it. A chief petty officer at that time got $99 a month, and if he was a permanent chief, he got $125 a month. Of course, we had no change in pay from 1922 to 1940. The pay remained the same.

Q: There was a decrease in there.

Admiral Walker: Yes, there was a 15% decrease under Roosevelt, and there was a 12.5% decrease under Hoover for a year.* He did it by having you take one month's leave without pay. Then Roosevelt came in and put it down to 15%. They said, "Oh, what a wonderful guy Roosevelt is."

I said, "How can you be so stupid? He's taking 15% of our pay, and Hoover only took 12."

Q: Well, I take it you could survive on what you were getting.

Admiral Walker: Not very well. Survive is the word. Survive.

---

*Herbert C. Hoover was President from 1929 to 1933; Franklin D. Roosevelt from 1933 to 1945.

Because I had no financial backing whatsoever. We just had to live on what came in. Miriam had a 1923 Ford coupe when I married her, and we took that out to Honolulu with us, and shortly after we got there, we made arrangements to get a new Ford Model A, which was delivered in July of '28. It was a light baby blue Ford roadster with a rumble seat on it. Boy, I loved that car. But we only kept it for about two years, and then her mother and father and uncle decided to come out and see us. But we couldn't get all those people in that Ford roadster, so we got a two-door Ford, which we had up to the time we left there in December of '31 to bring the R-boats back to decommission them in Philadelphia. And I turned that Ford in in Honolulu and bought a four-door Ford in Philadelphia.

Q: Describe how you made the approaches and attacks in that period.

Admiral Walker: Of course, we had no torpedo control system. We had two things. We had what they called an "is-was," which was just a couple of circles with a compass on them that you could set for your own course and also set for the angle on the bow of the target and from that, figure out the target's course. And we had what, as I remember, was a Mark 13 torpedo angle solver. And you set that up to find out what bearing to set your periscope on, to know when to fire the torpedo. And you'd just take as few observations as you could so that you wouldn't get sighted, because if you got sighted, you got penalized. We would run against the tender, named the Seagull.* She only would go about 12 knots. But once in a while we'd get some destroyers assigned to us and they would go up to 20 or 25 knots to train us in making high-speed approaches and zigzag approaches. Practically all the runs were zigzag runs, but at 10 or 12 knots, it wasn't too difficult, but we had the so-called attack teacher that we all used to practice attack techniques on. It was on the beach and simulated an attack on a ship with various models to put on the attack teacher to simulate the type of ship you were going to attack.

Q: How good did you get with these primitive methods?

Admiral Walker: Well, pretty good. When I commanded the S-boat, I think I got about 90% or better hits.

Q: That's impressive.

Admiral Walker: Yes.

---

*Even though the USS Seagull (AM-30) was officially designated a minesweeper, she served as a submarine tender at Pearl Harbor during the 1920s and 1930s.

Q: How frequently did you fire torpedoes?

Admiral Walker: Oh, maybe we would go out and practice seven or eight times, maybe fire twice a month. Sometimes we'd fire one or two. Sometimes we'd fire a whole salvo, but mostly we'd fire one or two at a time. In the S-boats and R-boats, we didn't have any stern tubes. We only had four tubes in the bow. Later, fleet boats had six tubes in the bow and four in the stern.

Q: The submarines pretty well had Pearl Harbor to themselves at that time, didn't they?

Admiral Walker: Pretty much. We had a division of about four destroyers there, and then during the winter, the Pacific Fleet generally came out there for a cruise, were out there for a little while.

Q: Did you train with them at all during those cruises?

Admiral Walker: Yes, we would train with them as they were coming in from the West Coast or when they were going back, we'd make attacks on them. But that's the only time we had really big targets to work with.

Q: What was the presumed mission of the submarine force in that era, to work with the fleet?

Admiral Walker: No, not too much. We couldn't keep up with the fleet. Our maximum speed was about 13 knots. Shore defensive submarines is what they were. The concept of maybe working with the fleet didn't come in until the fleet boats came in.

Q: You served in three different R-boats when you were out there. Can you differentiate?

Admiral Walker: I only served in one, the R-8, three and a half years in the R-8.

Q: The R-15 and R-13, where were they?

Admiral Walker: On the way back to Philadelphia, my classmate "Pilly" Lent was ordered from the R-15 to engineering PG and I, being an experienced engineer officer, they sent me over to the R-15, and I decommissioned the R-15.* As soon as I decommissioned the R-15, I was ordered to New London to the R-13. And she was a school boat, and I was in a school boat for one year. I was the third officer on the school boat. Sumner

---

*Lieutenant (junior grade) Willis A. Lent, USN, later a World War II submarine skipper and squadron commander.

Cheever, a mustang from World War I was the skipper.* Henry Eccles, you've heard of him, he was exec, and I was the third; Hamilton Stone was the fourth.** You know "Ham" Stone? Ever heard of him? My class.

Q: No.

Admiral Walker: And there, of course, we were out every day. We were taking part of the class out for training. If I didn't have anything to do that day, I could go to bed and they could sound the dive, and it didn't even wake me. I could sleep right through it.

Q: What brought about this decommissioning at Philadelphia after you brought the boats back?

Admiral Walker: They brought back all 20 of them, and then they sent out a couple of--well, I don't know how many went out, but they sent out S-boats. And when I got out there in 1935 after I finished my PG course, I was ordered to command the S-21. We had three divisions out there of S-boats, and I was in the Seventh Division. There was the Eighth Division and the Ninth Division,

---

*Lieutenant Sumner C. Cheever, USN. "Mustang" is a term used for a former enlisted man who has become a commissioned officer.
**Lieutenant Henry E. Eccles, USN, who later became a flag officer; Lieutenant (junior grade) Hamilton L. Stone, USN.

Walker #1 - 94

and each division had six boats. And shortly after I got there, the S-40 boats were ordered to Panama, so then the rest of the time, I was out there from '35, to '37, we had just two divisions of old S-boats there.

Q: What was involved in this decommissioning process? How thorough was that?

Admiral Walker: Well, you have to clean up everything inside, you know, and put preservative on all the metal surfaces, take the engines apart and clean them, and stow the pistons and the connecting rods and all that. You had to account for all your spares, supposedly so they could put them back in commission in a reasonable time. As a matter of fact, they did recommission the S-boats, which were decommissioned, one division of the Pearl Harbor S-boats was decommissioned in '37. I brought the S-31 back and decommissioned her in Philadelphia in '37.

Q: Some of those R-boats were put back into commission.

Admiral Walker: The R-boats were put back in commission, that's right, during World War II. So you could see everything had to be accounted for and supposed to be in such condition you could put the boat back together and operate it in a reasonable length of time.

There's a funny thing. While we were in the Philadelphia Navy Yard decommissioning R-boats, they were recommissioning the old O-12 to go up through the Arctic, you know. And they put in that big thing that supposedly they could turn like a bore and bore up through the ice and they'd always get air. She broke down so many times, I don't think that ever worked; I don't know. But I know the midshipmen squadron had to pick her up on one of their cruises and tow her because she broke down. But she had worse engines than we had. Terrible.

Q: Did the Bureau of Construction and Repair have some kind of a manual of instructions for this decommissioning process?

Admiral Walker: Yes, yes, and the Bureau of Engineering.

Q: How much help did you get from the shipyard?

Admiral Walker: Oh, practically none. They weren't interested in that at all, because there were no changes to be made in the boat. It was just a case of preserving what was there, and that was all. So very little help from the shipyard, except to be tied up at their piers and get light and electricity and water and air from the pier. That was about it.

Q: And you didn't have a lot of electronic equipment to take care of.

Admiral Walker: None, except the radio. We didn't even have sound that amounted to much. In the R-boats, when I first went in them, all we had for sound was a thing that came up on the bow. Maybe you've seen a picture from World War I. It came back with three prongs with sort of rubber ears on the end of them. That's all we had for sound. It didn't work. And then we had the SC tube. It was a tube that came up and out through the hull with two rubber balls on each end, and you could turn it from below and listen to that and center the sound in your head. You needed good binaural sense to operate it. Of course, there were no electronics. That was all just sound, no electronics involved. Of course, we had a gyro compass, and that was it. Before you could qualify, you had to learn to start the gyro compass. I qualified. You had to be in submarines a year to qualify. In those days, there was only one qualification, qualification for command. There was no qualified in submarines and then qualifying for command. In those days, there was just one qualification. I reported January of '28, and I was qualified for command in March of '29.

Q: That's when you got your dolphins?

Admiral Walker: Yes, that's correct.

Q: One of your classmates who was a submariner was Lewis Parks.*
Did you have any dealings with him in that period?

Admiral Walker: No, he wasn't out there, no. I didn't have any dealings with Lew Parks until I went back to PG school. I don't know, I think he had been submarining in China or the Canal Zone, or maybe the West Coast. I don't know where he went, but he wasn't out at Pearl. Yeah, I knew Lew. I knew Lew well.

Q: What do you recall from this period, then, when you were the school boat in New London, other than that the diving alarm wouldn't wake you up?

Admiral Walker: I don't recall too much, except it was interesting taking the boys out and teaching them how to dive the boat, how to make approaches, and that sort of thing. As I say, we were out practically every day—rain or shine, snow or sleet, whatever. It was also a little tricky teaching them how to make a landing in New London because there was a pretty heavy current running there in the Thames River, so there was quite a lot to teach them shiphandling.

Q: What was involved in a man moving his family from Hawaii to

---

*Lewis S. Parks, as a lieutenant commander, was commanding officer of the USS Pompano (SS-181) at the beginning of World War II and eventually became a rear admiral.

New London?

Admiral Walker: Well, of course, in those days you didn't have all this packing of cartons and so forth. All your china and everything came in barrels, and things like your tables and chairs, they were crated. And they didn't mind driving a nail right through the crate and into the table; that didn't bother them in the slightest. To talk about getting any recompense for that, just try and do it. They'd just laugh at you. In those days, the Navy was not personnel-conscious. Like they used to say, "If the Navy wanted you to have a wife, they'd have issued you one." That was their attitude about everything as far as personnel. Now, of course, the Navy bends over backwards to look after its people. They didn't stop to think they were ordering you someplace where there was no place for your family to stay or anything. That didn't worry them in the slightest. And now, of course, when they order you someplace, they designate somebody to look after you, and your commandant writes you a letter to tell you what it's all about. I arrived in Honolulu with a brand-new bride. I didn't know from nothing. But, fortunately, my skipper came down and met us and took us home. Otherwise, I don't know what I'd have done. I didn't have any money in my pocket. It was terrible.

Q: Would they pay your wife's transportation out there?

Admiral Walker: Yes, but minimum. We went out on the *City of Honolulu*, and our stateroom was way back aft, just over the screws, way down as low as you could get and have a stateroom, right on top of the screws. Minimum transportation, which in those days was $165 per person. And Miriam was not a good sailor, and it was not what I call a happy trip in many ways.

Q: Did your household goods travel in the same ship you did?

Admiral Walker: Oh, no. Oh, no. My household goods, I didn't have too much, because we didn't have anything, didn't own any furniture. And all we had was glassware, silverware, some china. And also in those days, they crated up that old Model T Ford in Boston and shipped it out to me along with the other odds and ends.

Q: Did the Navy pay for shipping your household goods?

Admiral Walker: Yes, they did. We only had a 7,200-pound allowance for an ensign in those days, so there wasn't too much you could ship. I told you that when we left that first house we went to, we went to this new house in a little court on the Ala Wai Canal. We went out and we bought rattan furniture. It was a little two-bedroom house right on the canal.

Q: Then do you sell the furniture back when you leave?

Admiral Walker: Yes, that's what we did. We sold it to somebody. I don't recall whom. But we didn't bring it back with us, no.

Q: Did you have to lug a fair amount of uniforms around with you in those days?

Admiral Walker: Yes. I think probably more than they do today because we wore our uniform all the time. Now in submarines, we could wear dungarees when we were in the boats, but otherwise, we'd have to wear whites. We had no such thing as khaki or anything in those days. And so you either wore blues or whites. We wore blues practically not at all in Honolulu. Fortunately, they had a big laundry run by what in those days we called ship's service. They call them Navy exchanges now. They laundered your white uniforms very reasonably, but even then you couldn't wear a uniform much more than one day, so you could see, you had to have a lot. I probably had pretty close to a dozen white uniforms. But my blue uniform inventory was just what I had when I graduated, two suits and I didn't have to add to it.

Q: You had to have the formal uniform?

Walker #1 - 101

Admiral Walker: I had to have my full-dress uniform with me at all times, yes. You had evening dress, and then you had the frock coat, and the plain dress trousers and the railroad dress trousers.

Q: And that big cocked hat and epaulettes.

Admiral Walker: Big cocked hat and epaulettes, sure. I've still got it downstairs.

Q: So that was a lot to lug around between duty stations.

Admiral Walker: It sure was. I had a great big trunk and then another small steamer trunk, and I carried all my clothes in those two trunks. Miriam had a wardrobe trunk full of her clothes in those days.

Q: Did you have much in the way of civilian clothes?

Admiral Walker: Almost nothing. Maybe had a couple pair of slacks and a couple of white shirts and a lightweight jacket. I don't remember any knitted shirts in those days at all. A bathing suit, of course. I don't know whether we wore shorts very much, either. I don't remember that we did. We might have. I don't think so.

Walker #1 - 102

Q: How much support did your submarine get from a tender?

Admiral Walker: We didn't have any tender. The submarine base was our tender. There was no tender out at Pearl at that time.

Q: I guess the Beaver got out there about the mid-Thirties and serviced the S-boats.

Admiral Walker: That's right, the Beaver was out there when I had command of the S-21, and we used to take the Beaver with us when we'd go down to Lahaina for operations. And we'd operate during the day and then in the evening, the skippers would go over to the Beaver and have a dinner and come back to the ship. She sent her boat around to pick us up. We got the tender's boat to take us to the beach, and we got our beer on the beach and then came back to the tender for dinner.

Q: We were talking about your period there serving the submarine school in New London. By the time you got back, then, they had the escape tower?

Admiral Walker: That is correct. Yes.

Q: And did you have to go through that training?

Admiral Walker: Yes, we did. Yes.

Q: Was the Momsen lung in use at that time?

Admiral Walker: That's right. We all had to train with the Momsen lung. As a matter of fact, Momsen was around there at that time.*

Q: Do you have any recollections of him personally?

Admiral Walker: Yes, I do. He was there in the school boats when I was going through submarine school. I remember he and a fellow by the name of Ives were always playing pool all the time at the lunch hour up in the BOQ.** He and Norm Ives. They were both in '20. But Momsen was a real nice guy. He was smart, and he was very pleasant. He was a real nice fellow. I never actually served with him, so I only knew him casually and had seen him around the BOQ there in New London and also later on when he was running the escape tank there in New London. As I recall, he was running it during that year that I was in the R-13.

Q: I would guess that just by virtue of this invention, he was

---
*Lieutenant Charles B. Momsen, USN.
**Lieutenant Norman S. Ives, USN. BOQ--bachelor officers' quarters.

very widely known in the submarine force.

Admiral Walker: Yes, he was. Yes, he was.

Q: The criticism I've heard is that people thought that the Momsen lung was the only way to get out, and they didn't work on breathing techniques without the lung.

Admiral Walker: That is correct, except he started doing it himself and trying to teach other people to do it, because I remember he used to come up from the 100-foot level without any lung. The rest of us had to use the lung, because we were training with the lung. But he'd come up from the 100-foot level without any lung. You had a 15-foot level, a 50-foot level, and 100-foot level.

Q: Why didn't more people try it without?

Admiral Walker: I don't know, except for the fact that we were being taught how to use the Momsen lung. We weren't in there on our own at all. We had instructors in with us at every level, showing us how to fit the Momsen lung. But we all did know that in an emergency, you could get out without one. Of course, the big thing is you have to learn to breathe out, because as the pressure gets lower, your lungs expand, and you've got to get rid of that air. That's the one big thing you have to learn. Now, with the Momsen lung, you didn't have to learn to do this because you were just breathing all the time and it automatically did it for you. But when you're coming up without one, then you've definitely got to breathe out.

Q: One of the officers you had later in the *Mayrant*, Larry Savadkin, used that technique to escape from the *Tang*.*

Admiral Walker: Yes. Yes. Where is Larry now, do you know?

Q: He lives down near Annapolis. I've spoken to him in the last month or so.

Admiral Walker: Yeah, I liked Larry. He was my engineer officer. He was blown right out of the hatch that morning when we were bombed. It actually didn't strike us, you know. The bomb slid right down the side of the ship, exploded underwater, and blew in the whole side of the ship. Everybody went on their can immediately. I remember that. I have a cervical disk problem now, and I had that operated on just after I retired. I had a problem before retirement but they didn't pay any attention

---

*Lieutenant Lawrence Savadkin, USN, escaped from the USS *Tang* (SS-306) after she was accidentally sunk by one of her own torpedoes on 24 October 1944. See Rear Admiral Richard H. O'Kane, USN, *Clear the Bridge! The War Patrols of the U.S.S. Tang* (Chicago: Rand McNally & Company, 1977).

to it. But it got worse, and so after I retired, I went back to Norfolk and they operated on my cervical disk. That's one reason that I'm now retired with a physical disability because of this cervical disk problem, and that's the time that Roosevelt got his purple heart.* In all the later destroyers, after the *Mayrant*, they built ports or windows in the bridge area, heavy glass, but we had great big windows. The explosion just blew those windows to smithereens and a piece of flying glass caught Roosevelt in the hand and wrist. He had a pretty big cut, and he had to have it sewed up. That's *ipso facto* a purple heart.

Q: Well, at least he earned it. Some people didn't.

Admiral Walker: Right. Oh, yeah, he got it all right, no doubt of that.

Q: Is there anything else you recall from that time in New London when you were in the school boat? Those were probably about the busiest operating times for any submarine during that period.

Admiral Walker: We also went to the Portsmouth Navy Yard in

---

*Lieutenant Franklin D. Roosevelt, Jr., USNR, was executive officer of the USS *Mayrant* (DD-402), when she was damaged by a near miss from a German Luftwaffe bomb off Sicily on 26 July 1943.

Kittery, Maine, for a two- or three-month overhaul. It was the middle of winter, and I remember it was very cold. The only other thing I remember, at the end of the year, Henry Eccles took over from our skipper, and we went to Annapolis to take the midshipmen out for a little trip. They didn't do anything, they were just observers when we dove, but we took out several groups of midshipmen so that they would know what a submarine was all about.

Q: Was there an active recruiting drive on? Was that the idea?

Admiral Walker: Not that I know of, no. I don't think so. No.

Q: What steps and procedures did you need to go through to get qualified for command of submarines?

Admiral Walker: You had to prove that you could dive the boat. You had to dive the boat, show how you did it and how you handled it. You had to prove that you could operate every piece of machinery on the submarine. You had to prove you could start the engines by yourself, including air-starting, and it wasn't automatic air-starting. It had an automatic air-starting system on the engine, but it didn't work. It was designed so that air pressure lifted up a valve that closed the fuel valve so fuel couldn't go into the cylinders at the same time that the air was.

Walker #1 - 108

If you put them both in together, you'd get an explosion and blow the cylinder head off. So the only way you could start those old NELSECO engines by air was to take and give her the air, get her rolling over, turn off the air quickly, and turn on the diesel oil. And you had to prove you could start both engines up that way. And as I say, you had to show them you could start the gyrocompass, you could operate the torpedo tubes, you could operate the pumps, you could operate the air manifolds, all that. Every piece of equipment, the switchboard, all that. You had to be able to operate every piece of machinery on the ship.

Q: And that's do it yourself, not just tell somebody how to do it.

Admiral Walker: Oh, no. You had to do it. And also, you had to know where all the lines were in the ship. I swear, when I got through, I knew where all the lines were better than the chief petty officer, the chief of the boat, did. I knew where everything was on that ship. I had to, because I didn't know what kind of questions they were going to ask me.

Q: Was the submarine force then considered an elite within the Navy? Was this sought after?

Admiral Walker: No, not really. No. I don't think the

Walker #1 - 109

submarine force became elite until the late Thirties, when they started building the fleet boats and paying them extra pay and so forth. In those days, as I say, when I had command, we didn't get any extra pay in '35 to '37. No, it wasn't considered an elite force, no.

Q: Was it something that people tried, on the other hand, to avoid?

Admiral Walker: No, not really. I think most of the people that went in enjoyed it very much. Most of them didn't make any attempt to get out of it. The big problem came when, after your first sea duty, then normally you went ashore for two years. And then the big thing was--who's going to get command when you go back to sea? And it was only, in effect, the elite, the boys with the best fitness reports, who got the best commands on that second tour of sea duty. Now, of course, with me, I had an extra year ashore because I took the postgraduate course, which was only two years. But in those days, they were just starting a system that every class, as soon as they completed their seven years of sea duty, would go to the PG school for what they called the general line course, and that's what I went to.* I was

---

*The Walkers' son was born on 23 January 1933 in the Annapolis Emergency Hospital during the course of the tour of duty at the Postgraduate School. The son is Edward K. Walker, Jr.; at the time of this interview, he was a rear admiral in the Naval Supply Corps, serving as Commander Naval Supply Systems Command and Chief of the Supply Corps.

Walker #1 - 110

ordered to PG school for the general line course. But you then had an opportunity to make a selection of what type of a technical PG you'd like, and I opted for ordnance PG. Well, out of my group, I think we had about, as I recall, 18 or 20 of us that were in the ordnance group. They only selected ten, and the strange part of it, the number 11 man, who didn't make it because I made it, because I was number ten, he became Chief of the Bureau of Ordnance.

Q: Who was that?

Admiral Walker: He was an aviator. P.D. Stroop.* He was number 11 and wasn't selected for ordnance PG. I was number ten and selected. He became Chief of the Bureau of Ordnance. This shows how things work. It's just crazy.

Q: What kinds of things did you study in this general line course?

Admiral Walker: Well, sort of a refresher course in main engineering subjects and in navigation, communications, math,

---

*In 1959, Rear Admiral Paul D. Stroop, USN, became first Chief of the Bureau of Naval Weapons, which was formed through an amalgamation of the Bureau of Ordnance with the Bureau of Aeronautics. He had previously served in the Bureau of Aeronautics. Admiral Stroop's oral history is in the Naval Institute collection.

Walker #1 - 111

meteorology, and metallurgy. Of course, we never had any metallurgy that amounted to anything as midshipmen, but we had good metallurgy courses in that general line course. And that's about the main thing, yes.

Q: Did you study tactics or strategy at all?

Admiral Walker: No. No.

Q: Was the presumption that you would learn those things on board ship?

Admiral Walker: That was it, yes. That was the presumption, or that you would learn later through correspondence courses or from the Naval War College.

Q: Did you take any of those?

Admiral Walker: No. You know, in my day, when I became lieutenant commander or senior to that, the only people that went to the War College were the people they didn't know what else to do with. Nobody else wanted them. The War College couldn't object, so they sent them down to the War College. That's right. That's the way it worked. If anybody wanted you to come to work for them, you couldn't go to the War College. If nobody wanted you, then they sent you to the War College.

Q: That doesn't say too much for the War College in that period.

Admiral Walker: No, no, it doesn't. Well, it doesn't say too much of the Navy as a whole of that period. I mean, the way they did things was crazy in many ways.

Q: Was the general line course primarily book study and lectures?

Admiral Walker: Right.

Q: Why did you get into ordnance as a technical specialty?

Admiral Walker: Well, it was the most prestigious kind of technical specialty at the time. That's why I wanted it.

Q: Did you aspire to be in the so-called gun club?

Admiral Walker: Well, no, but I aspired to be known as ordnance PG, because in those days, more admirals came out of ordnance PG than any other specialty. So I said, "Well, I might as well give myself the best chance."

Q: How was it that you got to make a choice? Did everybody get a choice?

Admiral Walker: Everybody had a choice when they first entered the general line school. They opted for engineering or communications or meteorology, ordnance. That's about all that I can remember.

Q: I would think, though, there would be so many slots to go around. You say ten in ordnance, so not everybody who wanted that could get it. How did they decide who got what?

Admiral Walker: Oh, they decided by how well you did in the general line school for that year. As far as I know, they picked the top ten that had the best record. Now, how much they also used your general record in making the pick, I don't know. But I do know that your ranking at the general line school had a lot to do with whether you were picked or not.

Q: How much time did you have to spend studying for that PG course, both the line and the ordnance?

Admiral Walker: It was rough. I studied somewhere in the neighborhood of 65 to 70 hours a week--almost to midnight every night except Friday night and Saturday night.

Q: Did you have adequate preparation, do you think, for that kind of a course?

Admiral Walker: Yes, I mean, we were used to studying hard in the Naval Academy, so I expected to study hard when I went there. I knew there would be a lot of hours involved, and we just didn't plan to do anything at all. We had to wear uniforms to school in those days--of course, whites in the summer and blues in the winter. We'd get home from school about 4:00 o'clock, and it wasn't a case of just being there for classes. You had to be there at 8:00 o'clock in the morning and you didn't get out 'til 4:00. You had an hour off for lunch from 12:00 to 1:00. And we lived in Eastport at that time. I'd get home about 4:15, 4:30, and I'd study up 'til nearly midnight every night except for time off for dinner. That's just routine.

Q: Was math a big part of that course?

Admiral Walker: Math was a big part, a big part. I forget now what the subject was, but when finally they got to talking about the curl of this and the curl of that, the curl of the other thing, that was over my head. I didn't know what they were talking about. I got lost. But we went through differential equations and all that stuff, you know. We had a very intensive course in physics, too, and electrical engineering.

Walker #1 - 115

Q: Did you get into the applications of these things as far as naval weapons?

Admiral Walker: No, no, and we made a point not to, because we were being trained as ordnance engineers, not as gunnery officers. And that's why we had a little trouble when the new Superintendent came in, Admiral Herrmann.* I had trouble with him because he wanted me to have the ordnance people learning all about operations, and so I told him, "The bureau says we're not training gunnery officers, we're training ordnance engineers." And then I told him one day, I said, "Admiral, I know what I'm talking about. I'm an ordnance engineer. You have a reputation as a top-flight gunnery officer. But you're not an ordnance engineer; I am." He didn't like it, but by that time I didn't give a damn.

Q: What was the idea that you would do with this education once you got it? How would you use it?

Admiral Walker: Well, I didn't know. But that's when I found out I could do a lot with it. I finished the first year in the summer of '34. I went to PG school in '32, the first year, '32

---

*Rear Admiral Ernest E. Herrmann, USN, Superintendent of the Naval Postgraduate School from 1950 to 1952. This discussion described by Admiral Walker took place when he headed the ordnance department under Admiral Herrmann.

and '33, was the line school. Then from '33 to '35 was your technical school. For the ordnance technical, a few went to universities right away, but most of us had one more year at the Naval Postgraduate School and then a year's practical work. We went around to all the ordnance installations that were on the East Coast and observed how they operated.

In summer of '34, I was ordered to the Bureau of Ordnance and was put in the fire control section. There had never been any fire control work at all done for submarines in the Bureau of Ordnance. The head of the fire control section of the Bureau of Ordnance asked me to draw up specifications for a torpedo fire control system using an analog computer and other instruments to go along with it. To the best of my knowledge and belief, I was the first officer who ever conceived the idea of generating a torpedo gyro angle rather than a periscope angle for firing torpedoes, which meant we had to put in torpedo angles that operated continuously all the time. And so actually, you know, it was just an extension of a gun fire control system. In a gun fire control system, you generate altitude, elevation, and azimuth. In submarines, it's all one plane, so all you have to do is generate azimuth, which in torpedoes means gyro angle. But we had to put in gyro angle spindles in the torpedo that could be turned continuously, and the first thing that happened when you fired the tube, the spindle was pulled out, and the torpedo left the tube. So I ran off those specifications and, as I said, the first time in history there had ever been any specifications written up for torpedo fire control system for submarines. I went on up to Long Island City and spent three or four months there at the Ford Instrument Company observing their work.* In the fall of '34, they brought in Lieutenant Commander Bennehoff, assigned him to the fire control section of BuOrd in charge of torpedo fire control.** I remember coming back in the fall one time, and I had a big argument with Bennehoff. He wasn't convinced that torpedo gyro angle was appropriate; he said that the torpedo data computer should be generating periscope angle like we'd always generated before, using the old Mark 13 torpedo angle solver. But I finally convinced him of this, and when he wrote the first specifications to go out to the fire control contractors, I think he sent it mostly to Arma. I don't think he sent them to the Ford Instrument Company. Anyway, the first Mark 1 torpedo fire control system was built by Arma Corporation.

Q: When you've got a completely new system like that, how do you convince people that that's superior to what you've been doing all along? How do you show them?

Admiral Walker: You have to talk. You have to talk convincingly.

---

*The Ford Instrument Company was already a supplier of components of gun fire control systems.
**Lieutenant Commander Olton R. Bennehoff, USN.

Walker #1 - 118

Q: When you don't even have a prototype, how do you show them it's going to work better?

Admiral Walker: Well, I don't know. As I say, I figured out for myself that was the best one, and I thought I had Bennehoff convinced. Then he almost wavered, and I talked with him some more, and the people who were making the decision, the head of the fire control and the chief of the bureau, were all surface fire control people. They had to take the word of the people that were running the torpedo desk, what was the best thing. That's the honest truth, they did.

Q: Did you have any submariners come in on your side to give you some support?

Admiral Walker: No. When I was relieved of command of the S-21 in 1937, then I was ordered to command the S-31, and brought her back to the East Coast to be decommissioned. I was supposed to make a deep dive off Panama. We had to have a submarine rescue vessel in attendance when we did it, but the day I was supposed to do that, one of the light cruisers ran aground on Castle Island.* So they took the submarine rescue vessel and sent her

---

*The USS Omaha (CL-4) went aground near Castle Island Light in the Bahamas on 19 July 1937. She was refloated on 29 July through the combined efforts of tugs, beach gear, and artificial waves kicked up by five destroyers.

to Castle Island to help get this light cruiser off the rocks of Castle Island. They sent me to New London to have the boat prepared for the deep dive. They had to rig all these battens and so forth to measure the compression of the boat as you went down. Of course, 200 feet was considered a deep dive. We only did that once in six years. Normally we didn't go below 100 or 120 feet. So after they had fixed me up, then I went out and I made a deep dive south of Long Island. I ran down to the depth of about 210 feet--everything was all right--and went back to New London and then on down to Philadelphia and decommissioned the S-31. That was in December of '37.* After the decommissioning, I was ordered to the Bureau of Ordnance. When I got to the Bureau of Ordnance, I was assigned to torpedo fire control in the fire control division of the Bureau of Ordnance. By that time, nobody was handling it. Bennehoff had left, and I came in.

So my main job was to write the specifications for the second procurement. In the fall of '38, they sent me to Panama in the USS Snapper, which was one of the first submarines to get the new Mark 1 torpedo fire control system. I was down there for a couple of months observing firing, and then I came back and wrote a report and made several suggestions that I thought should be made. And then I was given the job of writing the specifications and overseeing the design and procurement of the new system,

---

*A daughter, Helen Gail Walker, was born into the family on 10 November 1937 at the Lying in Hospital in Philadelphia. She is now Mrs. Charles Robert Reuning.

which was known as the torpedo fire control system Mark 2.

One thing I observed--there were very difficult communications between the officer in the conning tower and the officer operating the torpedo data computer in the control room. And I decided that what we needed was a torpedo data computer in the control room, and I recommended that, and they assigned an engineer from the design section of the Bureau of Ordnance to work with me. The engineer assigned to me was a Mr. Enright in the design section with the Bureau of Ordnance, and he was the one that conceived the idea of the torpedo data computer in the control room that fits the contour of the hull in the conning tower.

Q: Was this a naval officer, Enright?

Admiral Walker: No, he was a civilian engineer in the design section of the Bureau of Ordnance. And we got it approved with no problem, as far as I know. The only approval I ever had for it was from the head of the fire control section. I don't think the chief or the assistant chief gave a damn how it worked, but the head of the fire control section thought that was a good idea. He didn't know anything about submarines, anyway. He thought it was a good idea, so I had no problem putting it across. But then I wrote the specifications for the Mark 2 torpedo control system. In addition to that improvement, the original torpedo fire control system Mark 1 had a follow-the-pointer system for keeping the gyros set in the right direction. One pointer hooked to the gyros, the other one to the computer. You just matched the pointers. Well, in gun fire control, this was all done automatically by elevation indicator-regulators and azimuth indicator. So I said, "Let's put in an indicator-regulator in the torpedo control system." Because an indicator-regulator can do a much better job than any man can possibly do, and so we got that across. We also, with the help of Enright, we designed a periscope bearing transmitter by which we could transmit bearings directly from the periscope to the torpedo data computer. The whole weakness of the system was range. We didn't have any very satisfactory range finder for the periscope. We had a gadget that clipped onto the periscope which you could get a range, but it wasn't too accurate. But it was the best they had, and we had to do with that.

Q: That had to be fed in manually?

Admiral Walker: The commanding officer, he'd get the range and he'd say "5,200 yards," and the data computer officer was standing practically beside him, and he'd crank the 5,200 yards right into the computer. The only other input concerning the target was bearing. The periscope was raised from time to time to check the target's bearing. When he wanted to transmit the bearing of the target, he'd just press a button on the handle of the periscope, and that would transmit that bearing to the torpedo data computer. The submarine's course and speed were entered into the TDC automatically. With this information, the TDC continuously generated target range and bearing and also torpedo gyro angle for both the bow and stern tubes. The range and bearing of the target were checked visually or by sonar from time to time, and corrections were made on the target's estimated course and speed to bring them into line with the latest observations. As the war progressed, it became evident that night attacks by surfaced submarines using torpedoes against convoys were very efficient. Therefore, a target bearing transmitter was mounted on the bridge to aid in making these night attacks.

Q: Had you had any experience with analog computers before this?

Admiral Walker: Only a little bit with Ford Instrument Company on my PG course. Of course, I was listening to the talk all day long in the fire control section, because that was divided into main battery fire control and secondary battery control, including antiaircraft, mostly antiaircraft. There wasn't much secondary battery control, because by that time they'd practically forgotten about the old 5-inch/51 secondary battery, but everything was the antiaircraft guns. I was listening to that talk all day long, and so I picked up a lot that way.

Q: It's still a matter of trying to figure out the course and speed of the target and where he's likely to be.

Admiral Walker: That's right. And you knew that he was probably going to change. In most zigzag plans of most navies, they generally ran up to about six minutes on any one leg, but then you didn't know if he was going to turn right or left or how much. Most of the plans work out to give you at least 80% advance along the line you want to go. So that's about all you have to work with.

Q: So how do you work the zigzag idea into your TDC design?

Admiral Walker: Well, you just estimate the angle on the bow and crank that in along with the bearing and the range at the time. You get your range by just one bang from the sonar, one bang, that's all you need, one bang. You get better range with sonar than through the periscope. You could get the range with the sonar, but you took a chance you might get heard by the target's sound gear. But if you just took one bang, the chances were rather slight, and that was the best range you could get, the sonar range.

Walker #1 - 124

Q: So, in effect, what you did was adapt the surface gunfire mechanism to a completely different weapon, the torpedo.

Admiral Walker: That is correct. Now, when I was ordered to the bureau, I was responsible for all torpedo fire control, both surface and submarine. However, two years before that, Arleigh Burke had been down at the naval gun factory and had designed or been charged with design for a new torpedo director for destroyers and it worked out very well.* So I spent zero time on the destroyer torpedo fire control system.

I was also charged with minelaying. Well, my one contribution there was that I felt why spend all the money to get a timer for dropping mines that follows all Navy specifications as far as imperviousness to dampness and every other thing. I said, "It's just not going to be out in exposed position. Why don't we buy an ordinary commercial timer at about one-tenth the price?" And I talked them into that, and that's what we did. And the first minelayers that came out had commercial timers that we bought for them. That was the first minelayer that we built for World War II.** Now what they did after that, I don't know,

---

*Lieutenant Arleigh A. Burke, USN, who had a postgraduate ordnance engineering degree. Burke was later a noted destroyerman in World War II and Chief of Naval Operations from 1955 to 1961. The naval gun factory was in Washington, D.C., at what is now known as the Washington Navy Yard.
**The USS Terror (CM-5), commissioned in 1942, was the Navy's first and only built-for-the-purpose minelayer. Two ships intended to be sisters, Catskill (CM-6) and Ozark (CM-7), were converted to mine countermeasure ships.

but the first two had the timers that I had bought commercially.

Q: Was there anything in Burke's torpedo director for destroyers that you could use in the submarine TDC?

Admiral Walker: No, an entirely different type of thing. The Burke torpedo director was almost like a grandiose "is-was." It was just different and it didn't have any computing to it at all. There were no integrators and things like that in it.

Q: How well received was the new TDC by your fellow submariners?

Admiral Walker: Not very well at first. Most of them said, "I can fly better by the seat of my pants. I can do it better by bow and arrow." Well, they were just too goddamn lazy to go learn how to use it.

Q: How did they get convinced?

Admiral Walker: Well, the war finally convinced them, because with things moving so fast, you can't possibly--your mind and two people working together just can't work fast enough to make up and counteract all the different moves of enemy ships, especially when there's a lot of movement going on around you. When there's more than one, you've got to shift from one to the other. You just can't work that fast unless you have some kind of computer help. And so the skippers found that out, and it was unfortunate that there were a lot of bugs in the first ones that came out, and, of course, there must have been about 50 of them went out. There was only one group of ships got the Mark 2 that I wrote the specifications for. That was the Tambor class. The Mark 2 was built by Ford Instrument Company. When World War II started, they decided that Ford Instrument Company would concentrate entirely on surface fire control, and that Arma would concentrate on submarine fire control. And so they built a Mark 3, which was very, very much like the Mark 2. It still had the torpedo data computer up in the conning tower with the same configuration as the one we figured out for the Mark 2. And when I was naval inspector of ordnance in Ford Instrument Company for two and a half years during the war, I was also naval inspector of Arma, but I had an assistant inspector over there working. I didn't have to go over there except to say hello and drink a cup of coffee, because I had an assistant inspector working for me over there, a hell of a nice guy and a good man. But as I say, all the fire control equipment after the first six months were built by Arma. All the surface fire control equipment was all built by Ford.

Q: Do you think the bugs in the initial version were part of the problem of selling it to submariners?

Walker #1 - 127

Admiral Walker: I think so. Definitely, because I found the bugs out when I went on that first trip on the *Snapper* down to Panama in the fall of '38.

Q: What kind of difficulties were they?

Admiral Walker: Well, first of all, it had an automatic method of determining the course and speed of the enemy. In other words, you'd put in a bearing and range, and then you'd push in something that would start computing on the course that the ship was on at that time, and then you put in a bearing and range later and it would give you the course that the ship was on. But the ranging was so poor and they hadn't learned too much about using sonar to help them with the range, that it was just a useless appendage on there, just a pain in the neck. It wasn't helpful at all.

Q: Well, it's hard to blame these people, then, for being reluctant to accept it.

Admiral Walker: That's right. That's right.

Q: Where was the first mock-up or prototype made? Was that at Ford?

Admiral Walker: There never was a mock-up made that I know of. There was a drawing made. Ford made the drawing. No, the very first approximate drawing was made by Mr. Enright, who sent it up to Ford.

Q: Did you and he collaborate on what would go in this drawing?

Admiral Walker: Yes. As I said, they assigned him to work with me. I was responsible for the design procurement and so forth of the torpedo control systems.

Q: Maybe they knew you hadn't done too well in mechanical drawing at the Naval Academy.

Admiral Walker: Maybe, but I don't think it entered the picture.

Q: So you were able to tell him what you wanted to accomplish and he transmitted that to paper.

Admiral Walker: That is correct. That was the purpose of the civilian design engineers in the Bureau of Ordnance.

Q: I would think they'd have some kind of a test model before they went right into production, though, didn't they?

Admiral Walker: No, never did in those days. Never had any test models.

Q: The first one they built was going in a ship somewhere, then.

Admiral Walker: That's right. The art of building analog computers was so well developed for gun fire control that there was no worry about how well the torpedo data computer would work. The TDC was a much simpler machine than the gun fire control computers. We ordered six TDC Mark II systems for all the Tambor-class submarines.

Q: What kind of results did you get in the Snapper? Were they just sort of mediocre?

Admiral Walker: Yes, just mediocre. Very mediocre.

Q: Were people right in saying you could do as well by the seat of your pants?

Admiral Walker: No, they were not. It was better than that. They thought they could, but they couldn't. If it was a very simple problem, yes, they could do it. But if there were any complications involved, they couldn't. Because they just couldn't work fast enough. Their brains wouldn't work fast enough.

Q: What sorts of complications would make it a useful system?

Admiral Walker: Well, first, you've got to have continuous gryo angles for both the bow tubes and the stern tubes. You can't do that at all with a torpedo angle solver and setting the periscope. I mean, you just wouldn't have time to do it. And if you didn't have the system, it makes your bow and stern tubes only about 60% efficient. With this new system, you're getting a solution for both sets of tubes at all times. And as long as you're anywhere near the correct course and speed of the target, you're going to get hits.

Q: Admiral Furlong was Chief of the Bureau of Ordnance during that period.* Did you have any contact with him?

Admiral Walker: Very little. Hank Markland was number two man in the Bureau of Ordnance.** And when I first went to the Bureau, Bill Kitts was my boss in the fire control section.*** Then Al France relieved him, but he was a nice guy, too.**** They were both very good to work for.

---

*Admiral William R. Furlong, USN.
**Captain Henry T. Markland, USN, assistant to the Chief of the Bureau of Ordnance.
***Commander Willard A. Kitts III, USN.
****Commander Albert F. France, Jr., USN.

Q: Kitts went on to Admiral Kimmel's staff at the time you were in SubPac.*

Admiral Walker: That's right. Kitts had been a turret officer in the New York when Kimmel was the gunnery officer of the New York in the Fifth Battle Squadron in World War I.

Q: How much interchange was there between Bureau of Ordnance and the Division of Fleet Training in OpNav?

Admiral Walker: Practically none. Practically none. Our biggest problem in the Bureau of Ordnance was the torpedo section. We found that the torpedoes were so erratic on 90-degree turns that we had to advise all the skippers to turn the ship enough to bring the gyro angle as close to zero as possible, because you'd get a variation of 150 to 200 yards on advance of a torpedo on a 90-degree turn. And not only different torpedoes, but the same torpedo fired twice. One time it would go out about 150 yards and turn, the next time it would be 300 yards before it would turn. Well, it's awfully hard to get anything to hit with something like that. I never could convince the torpedo section that their torpedoes were so awful.

---

*Admiral Husband E. Kimmel, USN, Commander in Chief Pacific Fleet from February through December of 1941.

Q: And that doesn't even get into the question of whether they can explode or not.

Admiral Walker: Of course, the worst part with the torpedoes was the exploder mechanism. I well remember that the admiral sent me over to a tender which had come out to Pearl just before the attack on Pearl Harbor, and I had to go in and see the skipper most secretly to get a few of the new Mark 6 exploders for the submarines out there, the magnetic ones. Oh, it was terrible. That was the stupidest thing they ever did, to keep the Mark VI exploder so secret. Of course, torpedoes were expensive in those days. At least they thought they were. They cost $10,000, and the idea of firing a torpedo into a concrete wall or something and blowing up $10,000 just made people frantic. People down there in the Department of Defense now, they wouldn't worry at all. That wouldn't even be chicken feed.

Q: That's right.

Admiral Walker: But in the days that we were in there, when the Navy was run by the naval officers and not by civilians, it was different. And you didn't have any $1,000 hammers when the Navy was run by the naval officers.

Q: On the other hand, though, what you're saying is that they were too conservative.

Admiral Walker: They were, if anything, but not as far as things like spare parts and things like that. We made damn sure we got our money's worth, because look, in the middle Thirties when I was in the Navy, we ran the Army, the Navy, and the Marines on $1 billion a year. The Army got $600 million and the Navy got $400 million. Period. That's the way it was.

Q: And now you can get one ship for $1 billion.

Admiral Walker: You can hardly get one ship for $1 billion. And, of course, there was no separate Air Force. That was part of the Army appropriation, the Army Air Corps. But we ran the whole armed forces on $1 billion in the middle Thirties.

Q: Did you feel any other effects of that kind of stringent approach that you can cite examples of?

Admiral Walker: No. Like I said, we were very careful to get our money's worth out of anything we spent, because we only had so much. And something which I didn't know about at the time-- they were just experimenting with radar, and the boss of the fire control section, Kitts, gave them $100,000 of his allowance to help develop radar at that time, and he didn't tell me about it.

Walker #1 - 134

I never found out about it until later. He gave $100,000 of his budget to the communication guys to help develop radar. Of course, he could see that if it was ever developed, it would be wonderful for fire control.

Q: And that turned out to be the case.

Admiral Walker: That turned out to be the case. Yes, that sure did.

Q: Tell me more about your first command. You've just mentioned it a time or two in passing here.

Admiral Walker: Well, I went out and took command of the S-21 in June of 1935, at which time I was 30 years old. The ship had just been in overhaul to get a new lead lining for her battery tank. The other one had got a hole in it and acid started to eat a hole in the hull, so she went in the navy yard and got it fixed. So I wasn't able to have any turnover exercises going out with the other skipper to see how the boat operated. I just had to take it as is. And I'd never had a day's duty on an S-boat. All my duty had been in R-boats. So I had to be a little careful and learn how to dive the boat and just take it easy and work it out. After that, I had great fun. I never enjoyed anything more in two years in my life than I did in command of the S-21. The

S-21 was in Submarine Division Seven. Donald Dalton in '15 was my first division commander.* A little while after I took command of the S-21, he was relieved by Mike Ely in '17, a great guy and a good division commander.**

Q: What made that duty so enjoyable?

Admiral Walker: Well, I had good officers, I had a good crew, and I was the boss. That's what I liked best. That's what I work best at. I don't work well for other people.

Q: The satisfaction of being in charge.

Admiral Walker: That's right.

Q: How would you compare the S-boats in capability with the R-boats?

Admiral Walker: It was bigger and more comfortable, but other than that, there wasn't too much difference. They each had four torpedo tubes in the bow, and that was it. Period. The R-boats had a 3-inch gun, and the S-boats had a 4-inch gun, and I spent

---

*Lieutenant Commander Donald M. Dalton, USN, Commander Submarine Division Seven.
**Lieutenant Commander Harold F. Ely, USN, Commander Submarine Division Seven.

Walker #1 - 136

all my time when I was operations officer telling them to get rid of guns.* I said, "What the hell do you want with a gun on a submarine? A submarine that comes up to use the gun is stupid. If he takes one hit, he's no longer a submarine." You don't want guns on submarines; it's the stupidest thing that ever happened. They finally figured that out, and submarines today don't have any guns.

Q: It took a long time to make that change.

Admiral Walker: I know it. I mean, people don't use their heads. What good is a gun? As I said, one shot and it's no longer a submarine. So you don't want to use a gun. It's better to let the thing go, whatever it is, than go up and try to shoot at it.

Q: Well, I think that goes back to the idea we were just talking about, about economy. Bullets were cheaper than torpedoes.

Admiral Walker: Yes, that's right. I think that's probably it. Yes.

Q: Where did the S-21 operate when you had command?

---

*This refers to the period at the beginning of World War II when Walker, as a lieutenant commander, was operations officer on the Pacific Submarine Force staff.

Admiral Walker: Out of Pearl entirely, the whole time. We never went to the West Coast while I had command of her. We operated entirely out of Pearl. I brought the S-31 back to New London, made a deep dive, then took her to Philadelphia for decommissioning and went to the Bureau of Ordnance.

Q: What kind of range did the S-21 have in getting away from Pearl itself?

Admiral Walker: Oh, she was good for about 4,000 miles.

Q: Did you go that far?

Admiral Walker: No, no, no.

Q: How far would you go?

Admiral Walker: Well, we never went beyond the islands. We'd go down to Lahaina. A couple of times we went down to the big island, down to Hawaii, and then we went over to Nawiliwili once, I think. But otherwise, we operated right out of Pearl Harbor.

Q: Was this still a case of single-boat operations rather than coordinated?

Admiral Walker: Oh, yes. No coordination. Once in a while, you'd get an ex-surface man trying to teach you to do a column right and left, but we didn't pay any attention to that. We had little flags we'd put up when we got the signal.

Q: You said you had good officers. Any that particularly stand out in your mind?

Admiral Walker: Well, Underwood was with me.* He was quite a famous submariner. C.B. Stevens was with me; he was quite good.** He was the exec my first year in command. Tex Mewhinney was my second exec, and he was a crackerjack, and he had command of an S-boat during the war.*** Then there was J.E. Stevens.**** I had two Stevens boys. But they were all okay.

Q: What does a skipper do to keep these competitive, hard-charging guys working together for a common good?

Admiral Walker: Well, I don't know. I guess you just try to lead them on, to know what you're trying to do and what you want, and that's it.

---

*Lieutenant (junior grade) Gordon W. Underwood, USN. He was credited with sinking 14 Japanese ships as commanding officer of the USS Spadefish (SS-411) during World War II.
**Lieutenant (junior grade) Clyde B. Stevens, Jr., USN.
***Lieutenant Leonard S. Mewhinney, USN.
****Lieutenant (junior grade) James E. Stevens, USN.

Walker #1 - 139

Q: Were there any people you have worked for that you particularly admired as leaders and tried to use their style when you became a skipper?

Admiral Walker: Not particularly, no. Just a composite.

Q: What portion of your work as skipper was operational as opposed to administrative?

Admiral Walker: Oh, I would say 60% was operational and 40% administrative. Yes.

Q: Any startling lessons learned during that period?

Admiral Walker: No, I don't recall any. Mostly routine operations and the damn reports you had to be putting in all the time on everything under the sun you could think of.

Q: Well, weren't you able to leave that pretty much to the exec?

Admiral Walker: Yes, but you had to sign them; you had to look them over. I never was good at details.

Q: Did you get in any rough weather situations?

Walker #1 - 140

Admiral Walker: Only on that one trip from Pearl to San Diego in the R-boats in 1930 when it was so rough, that I told you about.

Q: How much support did your boat get from the tender Beaver when you were out there in the S-21?

Admiral Walker: We got no real support as such from the Beaver. All our repair operations were taken care of by the shops on the submarine base. However, several times she came with a group of submarines that were operating in Lahaina Roads, and she offered a place where the commanding officers could go over and get dinner and get together after the operations of the day. And she had boats that also could take us ashore to the village of Lahaina. The submarines had small skiffs that were nested under the deck of the sub, but they were difficult to get at and they weren't very safe in any sea of any kind. So we'd go over to the Beaver in her boats after the day's work and get together. Very often a group of us would stay over there for dinner. In addition to this, she made several cruises to the big island of Hawaii to take R and R cruises for the wives of the submarine officers, and, I think, also men, too, as I recall.* She'd take them down there, and they'd stay several days and come back.

In the spring of 1937, while I was in command of the S-21, we were part of an exercise for the defense of French Frigate

---

*R and R--rest and recreation.

Shoals, which is a little more than halfway between Oahu and Midway. I was assigned a patrol area that turned out to be excellent. The attacking carrier came right through my area. I picked her up as soon as she came over the horizon, traveling at high speed--about 30 knots--and zigzagging. I made a good approach and fired four water slugs at a range of about 1,000 yards. My division commander, Mike Ely in '17, was riding with me that day.

At the conclusion of the exercise, I received a dispatch from ComAirBaseFor, who as ComAirWhite was conducting the exercise. The interesting thing is that ComAirBaseFor was Ernest J. King, who was not noted for expressing appreciation.*

Q: You went from there back to the Bureau of Ordnance. Was there the idea then that if you had a PG education, a specialty, that you owed them so many tours in that specialty?

Admiral Walker: That is correct. After you had a specialty like an ordnance PG, they had first crack at you for all your shore

---

*ComAirBaseFor--Commander Aircraft Base Force. Admiral King's message, which was dated 11 May 1937, read as follows: "ComAirBaseFor as recent ComAirWhite [Commander Aircraft White Force in Fleet Problem XVIII] to whose command sail eighteen [USS S-18] and twenty one [USS S-21] were assigned wishes to express appreciation for fine work done by both ships in the service of security and attack at French Frigate Shoals."

At the time of the fleet problem, the S-18 was commanded by Lieutenant Richard G. Voge, USN, who later made a name for himself as operations officer on the staff of Commander Submarine Force Pacific Fleet in World War II.

duties from then on, at least until you got up to flag rank, if they wanted it. They had first crack at you, which turned out when I left the destroyer squadron command in Newport, the commanding officer of the base at Newport---Clarence Olsen asked me to come with him as his chief of staff, and I agreed to do so. But he sent in to get orders, and they came back and said, no, the Bureau of Ordnance was sending me to command the naval mine depot at Yorktown. So I never did become chief of staff of the commander of the naval base in Newport.

Q: Well, we've already talked briefly about your work on the subsequent developments of the TDC. What else did you do during that second tour in BuOrd?

Admiral Walker: That was my first tour. The other time was just a temporary duty as part of my PG course in the summer of '34. But this was my first assignment to the Bureau of Ordnance, and there, as I say, I worked all the time in the design and development of the new torpedo control system, Mark 2. And some time was spent in working on a mine timing device for the new minelayers. And that was about it, the whole time, except when they sent me for about three months to Panama on the Snapper to observe the new Mark 1 system to see how it was working and come back and make a report, which I did.

Q: Did there seem a particular sense of urgency at that time that war was approaching and you had to get ready?

Admiral Walker: Well, yes and no. There didn't seem to be any particular emergency as far as we were concerned, but there was a lot of worry over what was going on in Europe, and wondering if finally we were going to be concerned with all that. That was the time when everybody was sitting quiet, nothing was happening.

Q: Sitzkrieg, it was called.*

Admiral Walker: Yes, the sitzkrieg. That's right. And nothing was happening. So as I say, the day I was detached from the Bureau of Ordnance was the day that the Germans crashed through the Ardennes Forest in France and took over France shortly thereafter. And from then on, there was all kinds of worry about when we were going to get in it and how soon and in what manner.

Q: The German submarines had already begun a limited offensive by that point. Was there any emphasis on antisubmarine warfare in BuOrd?

Admiral Walker: I don't recall any. We didn't have really any

---

*"Sitzkrieg" was a sort of joking term to cover the period of relative German inactivity following the blitzkrieg period in September 1939. The "sitzkrieg" ended with the German advances into the low countries and France in the spring of 1940.

antisubmarine devices developed. You know, we had to use the British system when we finally got in. I forget what they called it.

Q: They had what they called an asdic.*

Admiral Walker: Well, it was the asdic but we had a different name for it then. Essentially what it was was a British asdic system we used. But there didn't seem to be anybody interested in developing any antisubmarine devices for the Bureau of Ordnance. Now I know when I was in command of the S-21, I sent in suggestions for antisubmarine search-and-destroy computer device, but it never got to first base in the bureau.

Q: How would you account for that?

Admiral Walker: I don't know. I've often wondered about that. I've often wondered about that. They just came back and, in effect, said, "Thank you very much. We have lots of suggestions for this type of weapon." That was it. No more than that. But they didn't have any. Because when I took command of a destroyer, all they had was this British asdic system in effect.

---

*Asdic was the British term for sonar, the underwater sound echo-ranging and listening device. Asdic took its name from the initials of the committee which developed it: Allied Submarine Detection Investigation Committee.

Walker #1 - 145

The destroyers weren't very interested in advanced techniques, I didn't think, or what we would call today high tech. They weren't interested in high tech in those days.

Q: I think you had partly the mentality of the old gun clubbers that the big gun was going to solve everything.

Admiral Walker: That's right. I think that was part of it.

Q: Was that kind of a tone set by Admiral Furlong from the top, do you think?

Admiral Walker: No, not necessarily. I think, if anything, he was more interested in the development of the antiaircraft systems than he was in the big gun systems, because, in effect, at that time, we didn't have any new big gun systems. The best thing we had was the Colorado class, which is the last one commissioned in '23, and they weren't building any new battleships until—well, I guess just when I was in the bureau at that time, they laid down the North Carolina.

Q: Right. Did you have any contact with Mike Schuyler, who was in the research division?*

---

*Captain Garrett L. Schuyler, USN.

Admiral Walker: Oh, yes.

Q: What do you remember about him?

Admiral Walker: Oh, I remember he was a character. The greatest thing I remember about Mike Schuyler was that he was always writing memos to files, and I often wonder what ever happened to all these memos to files, on a multitude of subjects. Whenever anything he would get interested in, he'd sit down and he'd write a memo to files, and they'd file it away. I often wondered whatever happened to all those memos to files. But mostly those were interesting things, you know, but instead of pushing them or talking about them, he'd just write a memo to files.

Q: Well, maybe he was more an idea man than an implementer.

Admiral Walker: That's right. He was. He was an idea man, there's no doubt about that. Yes, he was a good idea man. One time when he was range officer in Dahlgren Naval Proving Ground, he fired a shot right over the presidential yacht as she was coming up the Potomac. He never did live that down for quite a while.

Q: Were you getting any information from the Allied navies such as the British on what they were learning from the war, or was it too early?

Admiral Walker: It was too early. No, we weren't getting anything when I was in the Bureau of Ordnance that I can recall. And we figured at that time that we were far ahead in torpedo control systems of any navy in the world. Because we did have observers in the British Navy, but we never got any feedback on any new wonderful type of torpedo control system. And I don't think we captured any German ones until somewhere a couple of years later in the war, and even that wasn't in the same league with our system.

Q: How much of that credit should go to you? How much should go to the engineers of, say, Arma and Ford?

Admiral Walker: Oh, a lot should go to Arma and Ford because they worked out all the details from the specifications sent them by the Bureau of Ordnance. The complete design of the instruments, the internal mechanism and all how it worked, that was all done by the engineers at Ford and Arma. That wasn't done in the Bureau of Ordnance at all. We just put out specifications of what we wanted, what we wanted the inputs to be, and what we wanted the outputs to be. And it was up to them to figure out how to do it.

Q: But somebody has to have the idea.

Admiral Walker: That's right. You have to have the idea in writing and tell them what you want and what inputs you can give them and what you want to get out of it, and that's what we did in the bureau in those days.

Q: Did you find that there were things you could tell them you wanted that they were not able to achieve?

Admiral Walker: No. We were finding things that some of the engineers and people talked to me about that nobody seemed to be interested in. I talked to some of them, though I didn't promote it. But I always felt why did we still have torpedoes with an early 1900 design. The torpedo always ran with its rudder hard over. It was either hard right or hard left, so in effect, it zigzagged down the course. And I always said that with the modern sensors that we had and used in other fire control instruments, why couldn't we adapt that to the torpedo and get a torpedo that isn't overcompensating all the time? And finally I talked to Crook, who was the representative of Ford Instrument, into drawing up a plan to do it.* I don't remember if it was Ford or whether it was GE, but one of them, but it never did get anywhere.

---

*Ray Crook, vice president and Washington representative of the Ford Instrument Company.

Walker #1 - 149

Q: There was a new generation of fleet boats being built then at Electric Boat and Portsmouth. Did you go and visit those places to see about the way that your machine would fit in those?

Admiral Walker: I did go up to the trials of a couple of boats off Provincetown built by Electric Boat Company, now General Dynamics, to see how the Mark 2 torpedo fire control system did fit in, if everything was satisfactory. And I was on the trials as part of the trials inspection crew.

Q: Do you remember what boat you went out on?

Admiral Walker: I think it was the <u>Tambor</u>. That's the one I remember going out on.

Q: And what was your reaction?

Admiral Walker: I thought this was great. I didn't realize the bugs in the system until I went down to Panama in the <u>Snapper</u>. There just wasn't close enough communication between the skipper and the computer operator with the skipper up in the conning tower and the computer operator down below in the control room. And while they had telephones, the skipper wasn't going to use a telephone. They didn't have voice tubes, so the skipper would give the dope to his assistant approach officer, and the assistant approach officer would telephone it down to the data computer operator. It wasn't working out. The communication wasn't satisfactory. That's what made me come up and work with Enright to get everything together up in the conning tower for the new Mark 2 system.

Q: Well, when you got that and you went out in the Tambor and had that big change, had the bugs been pretty well wiped out in the system?

Admiral Walker: Yes, I think so. This was in the fall of 1939—December, I think. And the Tambor had the new indicator regulators for setting the gyro setting automatically. But there again, they didn't exercise the fire control system. They didn't do any approaching at all. They were just operating the equipment to see that it operated, mostly the engineering and diving equipment and that sort of thing. Sure, the computer was there, but there were no approaches made or anything like that.

Q: When did the feedback start coming in from approach trials?

Admiral Walker: When I was down in Panama. Not only was I down there on the Snapper, there were two or three other boats down there at the same time. I remember Karl Hensel from '23 had one boat down there at the same time.* I went out with him a couple of times.

Q: I mean after you got the modified version up in the conning tower, when did you start getting some feedback on how well that really worked in approaches?

Admiral Walker: Not until about the time I was leaving the Bureau of Ordnance in May 1940, because the Tambor wasn't commissioned until the spring of 1940.** She was on station off Wake when the Japs attacked Pearl Harbor, but she didn't do any shooting at all of any kind. And so then she went out on a war patrol, I think, in the Carolines, as I remember it. And she had several what she thought were good approaches and nothing happened. And we couldn't figure out exactly why, except that the setup wasn't as good as they thought it was. In hindsight, apparently it was bum torpedoes. But we didn't know it then. We didn't realize it. Everything was brand-new, just being used. And we were sinking some ships. If we weren't sinking any ships, we would have maybe thought a little bit more, but we were sinking some ships. How we were doing it, I don't know, now that I look back on it and read some of the things that happened after

---

*Lieutenant Commander Karl G. Hensel, USN, first commanding officer of the USS Seal (SS-183) when she went into commission in April 1937.
**The USS Tambor (SS-198) was commissioned 3 June 1940 with Lieutenant Commander John M. Murray, Jr., USN, in command.

I left, because I left in August of '42. So I don't know. But those torpedo exploders were really no good. But, of course, you didn't have anybody to tell you, except the skipper himself, and you never knew just how much credibility to put into what he was telling you. Because it's a lot different, say, looking at it from a submarine periscope and watching them go than it would be, say, from aircraft observation overhead, and watching what happened in the run of the torpedo. But we didn't have planes up overhead watching all this for us, to tell us that the torpedoes were hitting the sides of the ships and bouncing off.

Q: And it turned out that not only were some of the torpedoes not good, some of the skippers weren't either.

Admiral Walker: Oh, yes, sure.

Q: And so you had to sort out a lot of variables.

Admiral Walker: Lots of variables. It was hard to tell which was the controlling variable. And we had no reason to suspect that the system was all bad, that the Mark 6 was all bad, especially the electronic part of it, which was all new and nobody knew anything about it really, because they just threw it at us and said, "Here it is. It's been tested and it's good. It works. It's wonderful. We'll blow up the world with it." Well,

Walker #1 - 153

phooey.

Q: Did you request that assignment on the submarine staff?

Admiral Walker: When I was completing my tour of duty in Washington in the Bureau of Ordnance, I asked for command of a submarine, and I was scheduled to take command of the <u>Tautog</u>. But then Charlie Lockwood, had been over in the CNO's office, and he knew that I had been working in developing torpedo control systems.* He was ordered to be chief of staff to Admiral Friedell, who was Commander Submarines U.S. Fleet then.** So he wrote back and said he wanted me sent out to be gunnery and torpedo officer of the submarine force. So they cancelled by orders to the <u>Tautog</u> and sent me to the big staff. So that's how I got on the big staff, all because of Charlie Lockwood.

Q: Given the benefit of hindsight, would you have preferred to have the submarine command?

Admiral Walker: I think so. I don't know. I'm very happy with how things turned out.

---
*Commander Charles A. Lockwood, Jr., USN, was involved in submarine matters while serving in OpNav from 1937 to 1939. In 1939, as a captain, he reported as chief of staff to Commander Submarine Force U.S. Fleet. As a vice admiral, Lockwood served from 1943 to 1945 as Commander Submarine Force Pacific Fleet.
**Rear Admiral Wilhelm L. Friedell, USN, Commander Submarine Force U.S. Fleet.

Q: It's good that you can be that way.

Admiral Walker: I'm not too introspective about those things. They don't upset me too much. I take life pretty much as it comes, always have.

Q: Well, describe your arrival then on the staff. I think you were in the Richmond at the time, weren't you?

Admiral Walker: Yes, we were in the Richmond at the time, and she was in Honolulu. And I took a train across the continent to San Diego, then picked up the carrier Yorktown for transportion to Pearl Harbor. The Yorktown had hardly any planes on it. She was loaded with fire engines and all kinds of work. The whole flight deck was just covered with junk she was taking out to Pearl. I got out there and reported to staff. Of course, then I had over a year of just routine peacetime work checking the submarines' torpedo firing reports. First they went through the division commander and the squadron commander, and then they came up through me. That was a detail I didn't like that very much. That was too much detail for me.

Q: That was a pretty good-sized staff to be in a light cruiser, wasn't it?

Admiral Walker: Yes, it was. I told you who was on it. Charlie Lockwood was the chief of staff, Joe Connolly was the operations officer, "Dutch" Will was the engineer, Fitzwilliam was the communicator, "Weary" Wilkins was the flag secretary, and Ev Gunther in '26 was flag lieutenant.* That takes care of everyone. And I was gunnery and torpedo.

Q: Was it just a case of not having enough tenders available that you weren't in a tender?

Admiral Walker: No. The point was, see, we were responsible for all submarines in the U.S. Fleet, and we used to make the grand tour every year. We inspected the submarines in Pearl Harbor, then we'd go to San Diego and inspect submarines there. Then we'd go to Coco Solo and inspect the submarines there. Then we'd go to New London and inspect the submarines there. I reported in about June of '40 and about September we started on the grand tour, and we ended up in New London somewhere probably around the latter part of November.** Then we went straight back through the canal up to San Diego and had Christmas in San Diego. I knew we were going back to Pearl, so I sent a letter to Miriam asking

---
*Captain Charles A. Lockwood, Jr., USN; Lieutenant Commander Joseph A. Connolly, USN; Lieutenant Commander John M. Will, USN; Lieutenant Albert E. Fitzwilliam, USN; Lieutenant Commander Charles W. Wilkins, USN; Lieutenant Louis E. Gunther, USN.
　**During fleet problems, the Richmond was employed as a cruiser rather than operating with the submarines.

her to come on out to San Diego and bring the children with her. She'd been living with her mother. Of course, my home port was San Diego at the time, and she didn't know anybody there, so she didn't come out to San Diego when I reported to the <u>Richmond</u>. It wouldn't do any good because we were sitting most of the time in Honolulu, so it wouldn't do her any good to be sitting in San Diego. So she had stayed home. So she came out to San Diego for Christmas, and we had Christmas together. Then the admiral decided that he wanted me out at Pearl ahead of time for some reason. I don't remember if I had been promoted then to operations officer or not. I think I had been. There were conferences of the operations officers of all the various forces out in Pearl, and he wanted me there. So he sent me out on one of the old Navy tankers. I can't even remember the name of her now. And then Miriam came out later on a passenger boat. But since my home port was in San Diego, I had to bring her to Honolulu at my own expense and the children. Then when they got there, we had no place to live, so we rented this house, unfurnished, and then we went out and rented furniture, and that's all we had. She got out there in about the latter part of January of 1941.

Q: You had three separate tours of duty in Hawaii. What changes did you see over that period?

Walker #1 - 157

Admiral Walker: It was just amazing, the amount of building that went on, especially in the beach area. New hotels were added; houses were being built across Kalakaua Avenue. A lot of houses were built out in the Black Point area, and out in the area known as Kahala between Black Point and the Waialae Country Club. The building continued during our third tour, right up to the start of the war.

We didn't go back again until the 30th reunion of the Pearl Harbor survivors in December of 1971, and then the change from when we left in 1942 to 1971, actually, almost 1972, in that 30 years was just amazing. I couldn't even count the number of new hotels. The old Halekulani was still there. The Royal Hawaiian was so surrounded by high-rise hotels, you could hardly find it. The old Moana with the old banyan tree was still there. Constructed like it was, I was always a little worried about it because of fire, but as far as I know, it's still there and going strong.

Q: Was that a good place to have children out there, as you did in the early Forties?

Admiral Walker: It was a wonderful place to raise children. The climate in Hawaii is just wonderful. It runs in the low to middle 80s all the time, except once in a while when you have the so-called kona weather when the wind comes in from the south, and then it's sort of hot and muggy because we don't have the trade winds. But we used to take our son Ted to the beach when we lived out there, '35 to '37. He was just over two years old, and we used to swim all the time at Fort DeRussy. We had a little life ring, and we put that around him, pushed him out to the swimming raft; he'd kick around and he had a wonderful time. He learned not to fear the water at all, fortunately. However, he almost drowned except for Red Ramage.* In the fall of 1941, we had a staff party of the submarine staff at the Kalama Beach Club, which is on the windward north side of the island, and not far from the Kaneohe air station. We were there getting set up, getting the tables out from under the club house. The children went down in the water, and my son, who at that time was eight years old, was out with the Cromwell boy, young John Cromwell, who was two or three years older than he was. And the two of them got caught in the undertow, which was almost unknown there. They were being swept out to sea. Well, Cromwell tried to help Ted, was holding him up and so forth, but he wasn't making the grade. I guess he had to let go for fear he wouldn't make it. And Red Ramage, who was on the beach at that time and was coming down with a surfboard, saw the problem and raced into the water with his board and paddled out and got Ted, put him on the

---

*Lieutenant Lawson P. Ramage, USN. Ramage eventually retired as a vice admiral. His oral history is in the Naval Institute collection.

surfboard and brought him back into shore. And just about that time, I got down to the shore. Somebody yelled at me, and so when Ted came out, I picked him up in the middle with his head and feet down, shook him, and out came all kinds of water out of his lungs. He never passed out, but we were somewhat worried about him, so we immediately took him to the Children's Hospital in Honolulu, and he stayed in the Children's Hospital in Honolulu for a couple of days until they said his lungs were all clear and he was okay.

Q: One admiral saving a future admiral.

Admiral Walker: That's right. Yes.

Q: When was the submarine force commander moved ashore?

Admiral Walker: I think it was around February, around that time, that they organized a new Atlantic Fleet, got rid of the Scouting Force as such, and they in effect disbanded the U.S. Fleet, and we had the Atlantic Fleet and Pacific.* So we became Commander Submarines Pacific Fleet and the other command was Commander Submarines Asiatic Fleet, which we had no

---

*These changes were effective on 1 February 1941, when Admiral Husband E. Kimmel, USN, became Commander in Chief Pacific Fleet. Because the separate fleets were no longer expected to operate together, Kimmel's other title of Commander in Chief U.S. Fleet was a nominal one.

responsibility for at all. So at about that time, they took us off the Richmond and put us on the beach there at the submarine base at Pearl Harbor. It was also about that time, in February of '41, that we got the first orders of what to do in case of a Jap attack. It was all spelled out very carefully what everybody would do.

Q: Where did these come from, OpNav?

Admiral Walker: No, they came from, as I remember, Commander in Chief Pacific Fleet. People say nobody had given any thought to this. Well, that's not true, because the orders about what we should do in case of attack were way back then. I don't think they were expecting a surprise attack on Sunday morning.

Q: No, I think you're right there.

Admiral Walker: But they were expecting or assumed that there might be an attack as soon as war was declared. Because, as you may remember, as soon as they thought that the Jap fleet was going down into Sumatra or the Philippines, they then relaxed a little bit--another point, we had not too many of the PBYs that could scout out to 250, 300 miles. Well, they took a number of those away from us to send to Europe. I mean, we were being robbed all the time of equipment to send over to Europe. And

Walker #1 - 161

thus, we were not able to scout, say, that morning like we would have been if we'd had the number of planes we were supposed to have.

Q: What kinds of things were you doing on this grand tour that you mentioned?

Admiral Walker: We were just inspecting the bases and at each base, we would pick one or two boats at random and take them out for a day's inspection--diving, torpedo firing, all kinds of things.

Q: Generally what kind of condition were they, as far as war-readiness at that point?

Admiral Walker: They were as good as they'd ever be. They never were ready for the type of war that we were going to have.

Q: So these were still the old boats, not the fleet boats.

Admiral Walker: Yes. We had S-boats at Honolulu at that time, and we had a few of the new P-class that had come out, and were stationed at Pearl. We had a few of those around Pearl just before the war, but all S-boats in San Diego, all S-boats in Coco Solo, and all S-boats and O-boats or R-boats--at that time, it

Walker #1 - 162

was still the O-boats at the school in New London.

Q: Were you concerned about material condition in these when you made your inspections?

Admiral Walker: Yes.

Q: And the extent of training, I presume.

Admiral Walker: Yes, that's it. Material condition, training, that was it.

Q: Did you get much into tactics and doctrine in these visits?

Admiral Walker: No, no. But that was an individual thing. Each submarine was, in effect, trained individually by its own division commander. He checked on the boats, how well they were doing in actual firing, how well they were doing on tactics and things like that.

Q: Well, doctrine wouldn't be individual. How would that come about?

Admiral Walker: Well, there wasn't too much, as I recall. We never had any written doctrine as such. Well, we did have a priority. That was before the unlimited warfare was initiated.

We had priority of targets—major capital ships first, then cruisers and destroyers and so forth, the train ships.

Q: Was there much thought given to attacking merchant ships at that point?

Admiral Walker: None. No.

Q: Was there any idea of working together with the Battle Force units in coordinated tactics?

Admiral Walker: Not until we got a few of the P-boats, because the S-boats just couldn't keep up. No way you could work with them. And that's one reason they built the so-called fleet boats, because they had four diesels, and it was diesel electric power and they could make 21 knots when they hooked on all four. That was one of the reasons they were building fleet boats so they could operate with the fleet, operate out ahead of them, in effect, as screens. But we only had one division at that time, just the P-boats. And they weren't organized and worked up enough to really do that kind of work. They were just learning how to run their boats themselves.

Q: I imagine at that point it was still premature to know what qualities really would make a good wartime skipper, because you hadn't had any tests yet.

Admiral Walker: No, no. As I say, they thought at first that maybe some of the older skippers weren't aggressive enough, and that's when they decided to go in for youth. And also, the same thing had happened in England. They got rid of all their older skippers and put in all younger skippers. Lockwood, as I remember, sent W.R. Headden of my class over there to cruise around on one of the English subs.* And we were getting word back. Youth was the thing for submarine command.

Q: What impressions did you have of Admiral Friedell as the force commander?

Admiral Walker: He was a very nice old father figure, just a real nice old man. He was an ordnance PG, too.

Q: How was he as an aggressive force leader?

Admiral Walker: He wasn't particularly aggressive in any way. Lockwood was the mainspring of that staff. I remember we were out acting as a target. The submarines were out having torpedo firing practice, and they were using the cruisers' OUs there, little floatplanes to observe, and Charlie Lockwood dressed down

---

*Lieutenant Commander William R. Headden, USN.

the whole staff, because none of us were volunteering to go out and ride those planes. He went out two or three times himself, but nobody else was volunteering to do it.

Q: Sounds like he was very forward-thinking and aggressive.

Admiral Walker: He was, definitely. And he had a nice personality. He was really quite a guy, Charlie Lockwood was. I was very fond of him when I was on the staff with him.

Q: Then Admiral Withers came in after him.* What qualities do you remember of him?

Admiral Walker: He was sort of negative. I mean, he was a live-and-let-live type of guy. He wasn't forward-thinking or progressive at all. He just wanted everything to run smoothly and not bother him too much.

Q: Well, if you've got a guy like Lockwood that's willing to run with the ball, that's fine, isn't it?

Admiral Walker: Yes, except that Lockwood left about the time Withers came, and we got "Gin" Styer.** "Gin" was that way some,

---
*Rear Admiral Thomas Withers, USN, Commander Submarines, Scouting Force, Pacific Fleet.
**Commander Charles W. Styer, USN, chief of staff.

Walker #1 - 166

too, but Gin didn't have the personality of Lockwood. I never got along too well with Gin. I didn't trust him too much, and I don't think he trusted me. It wasn't too happy a situation. I don't know--that's my own feeling. He may have thought I was a great guy, I don't know.

Q: What tasks were you involved in in your own particular specialty, that is, in torpedoes and gunnery? What projects did you push?

Admiral Walker: There wasn't much pushing except to organize schools and give lectures on the torpedo data computer, trying to sell the use of the torpedo data computers to the commanding officers. That's the main thing I was trying to do. And, of course, I had quite a lot of detailed work working out the operations schedules and dovetailing them in with all the other forces at Pearl, all during 1941 'til the war came. And then after the war came, then one of my first jobs, I had to plot all the routes from Pearl Harbor to the various points that we were going to have for operating areas around Japan, and we decided we should keep the submarines at least 60 miles apart, so if they met with another submarine they wouldn't have too much worry about identification. They could figure that it was enemy if they inadvertently ran into another submarine either going or coming. And we left it quite a bit up to the discretion of the commanding officers on how far they should go on the surface and when they should start running submerged in the daytime and just running on the surface at night. That left very much to the conditions as noted by the individual submarine commanding officer.

Q: This must have been after you became the operations officer.

Admiral Walker: That is correct. Yes. I became operations officer in the spring of '41.

Q: Now we're talking about this grand tour. That had you at sea quite a bit. Did you spell any of the ship's officers on watches just to keep your hand in?

Admiral Walker: No. I spent most my time working up and checking these torpedo firing reports. We'd get a whole batch of them before we left that had to be checked before they were sent in to the Fleet Training people in Washington.* That was my job to check those things. That's what kept me busy all day. I used to play bridge with the exec and a couple of other officers at night, every night practically, we played bridge.

---

*The Fleet Training Division (OP-22) in OpNav was concerned with tactical training of the fleet. It relied on reports from the operating forces as a measure of readiness for war.

Q: Willis Lee was heading up Fleet Training back in Washington at that time. Did you have any dealings with him?*

Admiral Walker: None whatsoever. No.

Q: The Squalus had gone down the year before.

Admiral Walker: That's right.

Q: When you got up to that area, was there any feedback or holdover from that? Were people still buzzing about it?

Admiral Walker: I don't recall too much. I don't recall too much. I knew Naquin very well, the skipper of the Squalus.** One of the strangest things in our class when the war started was Mort Mumma, he had one of the 40 boats, and then he was sent to China, and while he was there in Pearl, he got the name of Captain Bligh because he was so rough on his crew.*** He made

---

*Captain/Rear Admiral Willis A. Lee, Jr., USN, was director of the Fleet Training Division until it was merged into the CominCh organization shortly after the United States got into World War II.
 **Lieutenant Oliver F. Naquin, USN, was commanding officer of the USS Squalus (SS-192) when she was commissioned on 1 March 1939. She sank off the Isle of Shoals on 23 May of that year. There were 33 survivors, including Lieutenant Naquin; 26 crew members were lost.
 ***Lieutenant Commander Morton C. Mumma, Jr., USN, was commanding officer when the same submarine, by then raised and repaired, was recommissioned on 15 May 1940 as the USS Sailfish.

one short patrol after the war started and came in and asked to be relieved. We never could figure that one out. It was strange. He was very rough and tough on his crew. Apparently, the excitement or whatever it was of the war just unnerved him, and at least he was smart enough to know he was no good and asked to be relieved.

Q: You say you knew Naquin well. What kind of a guy was he?

Admiral Walker: Well, Naquin is hard to describe. A lot of people thought he was sort of one-way, you know, in other words, everything for Naquin. He wasn't too much of a mixer.

Q: What kind of qualities did you look for in skippers? Did the force commander have any say in picking them?

Admiral Walker: Oh, yes, he did.

Q: Did you look for the rugged individualist type?

Admiral Walker: Well, we looked for people that were recommended by their commanding officer as being well-qualified and aggressive and would make good submarine skippers. They would send in their recommendation to ComSubPac, and then he would send a dispatch to the Bureau of Navigation and get them ordered to command.* That's the way it happened.

Q: What do you remember about the outset of the war itself?

Admiral Walker: Just before 8:00 o'clock Sunday morning, I was sleeping peacefully at home in Honolulu, and our home was not far from the big secondary school there that the missionary started, the Punahou School. And I heard this the noise of bombs exploding, and I said to my wife, "What's the Army doing having bombing practice on Sunday morning and waking up a hard-working naval officer at 8:00 o'clock on Sunday morning?"

About that time, the telephone rang, and it was Ed Swinburne, who'd had the duty that night at Pearl Harbor.** He said, "Get out here as fast as you can. The Japs are bombing Pearl Harbor."

Right across the court from me was a classmate of mine, Eddie Beck, who had just taken command of a new destroyer.*** He'd had an old four-piper and had just taken command of a new destroyer that Saturday, and he'd been out pretty much on the night before celebrating his new command. So I sent Ted over to wake him up and get him going.**** Then I called Ev Gunther, who didn't have

---

*The Bureau of Navigation issued officers' orders at that time. It was renamed the Bureau of Naval Personnel shortly after the beginning of World War II.
**Lieutenant Commander Edwin R. Swinburne, USN, who was on the submarine force staff.
***Lieutenant Commander Edward L. Beck, USN, commanding officer of the USS Phelps (DD-360).
****Ted is Walker's son, Edward K. Walker, Jr., born 3 January 1933.

a car.* I had two cars. I had a Buick, and also I had an old wreck. So I called Ev.

As I called on the telephone for Ev Gunther, I heard this woman say, "Oh, oh, this is awful. The bombs!" Apparently our telephone line had got crossed with somebody else up on the hill when some Jap plane had dropped a bomb up in the hills.

So I told Ev I was leaving just as soon as I could get some clothes on, and I'd be over to pick him up, and I did. Then we started out for Pearl. In those days there were cane fields on both sides of the road to Pearl, and I said to these boys, "Well, if any planes start to strafe the road here, I'm going in the ditch." Well, they didn't, but just as I got to the submarine base gate at Pearl Harbor, and the car window on my side was open, a Marine sentry said, "Watch out!" I pulled back and a big piece of shrapnel came in through the window and bounced on the other side of the car and fell to the floor. I've still got that piece of shrapnel somewhere. I don't know where it is. I said to the others, "Boy, that would have really given me a good shave." It was a piece of shrapnel from our own guns; that is what it was. And then I went in.

Eddie Beck, my classmate--his ship had already gone to sea, so he got aboard some other destroyer and went off to sea. And,

---

*Lieutenant Louis Everett Gunther, USN, flag lieutenant on Admiral Withers's submarine force staff.

of course, Ev Gunther and I stayed on the submarine base. I didn't get home again until after Christmas.

Q: What did you do all that time?

Admiral Walker: Well, I lived at the BOQ, and, of course, we were standing watches 24 hours a day, working all day and at least one watch at night.* Maybe we'd have one or two division commanders in as watch officers, and I was a watch officer. I remember about the second night after Pearl Harbor, we all had been issued revolvers and so forth by that time. I was coming out of the BOQ about midnight, and it was raining like the dickens, and somehow it short-circuited a transformer station not too far away. Sparks were flying. My God, everybody in the world began shooting at this thing. I just walked back into the BOQ and waited until the shooting was over. Of course, we had to carry flashlights with purple paper, just a little spothole in the middle so you could see where you were going.

Q: You had been sending out some boats on patrols even before that, say, to Midway and Wake.

Admiral Walker: That's right. We had been patrolling Midway since about October or November and also Wake. We had two boats

---

*BOQ—bachelor officers' quarters.

patrolling Wake, and I think we had three patrolling Midway.

Q: What was the purpose of those?

Admiral Walker: Just to report anything that came in and keep an eye open if something happened. Of course, when the Japs came, they came in force and the patrolling submarines didn't get in an attack.

Admiral Walker: Before the war started, they were all set to shoot. Their torpedoes were all armed and everything, and they had operational exploders in all their warheads and all that. But they were just to report to us anything that happened in those areas. We didn't know what might be happening. We had, of course, a number of Marines on Wake, and they were building a base and also building a base at Midway. So it was up to a month or a month and a half before Pearl Harbor that we had those boats on search, as I recall.

Q: How good was the logistic support at Hawaii for the submarine force?

Admiral Walker: It was excellent. It was excellent. We had a really good supply department there, well-stocked, we had plenty of food. Of course, one of the big things that Admiral Withers did was to lease the Royal Hawaiian Hotel as a rest and recreation facility for submarines as they came back to Pearl from war patrols. And that was really the first time in all my years in the Navy up to that time, which was about 17, that I had ever seen the Navy seem to give any regard to the personnel, real regard for the personnel. But Admiral Withers was that way.

Q: Where did this spark? Where did the idea come for doing that? Do you have any idea?

Admiral Walker: From Admiral Withers. He got the permission from Admiral Nimitz to do it.* I guess he had to get permission from somebody back in the Navy Department, too, but he got Admiral Nimitz's okay to go to the Navy Department and get the money to do it.

Q: What was your first awareness of the capabilities of Ultra, the code-breaking system?

Admiral Walker: Even though I was operations officer, I didn't hear anything much about it until about the middle of May, when I began to hear rumors that we were reading Jap dispatches.

---

*Admiral Chester W. Nimitz, USN, became Commander in Chief Pacific Fleet at the end of December 1941.

Q: May 1941?

Admiral Walker: No, May 1942.

Q: That long?

Admiral Walker: Yes, May 1942 was the first time I had any idea of that.

Q: That's amazing.

Admiral Walker: No, they weren't telling us. No, I never did know it 'til then.

Q: Well, I guess it would have been Withers and English after him; were they handling this personally?*

Admiral Walker: Yes. Once in a while they'd tell me to do something and I'd just wonder why, but they never did give any explanation.

Q: And you didn't ask?

---

*Rear Admiral Robert H. English, USN, relieved Admiral Withers as Commander Submarines Pacific in the spring of 1942.

Admiral Walker: No. No. So I began to hear that they knew exactly where the Jap fleet was coming, and the chief of staff asked me to draw up a plan for what we'd do with the boats. Well, the dope we got from the big staff was that the main force was coming in from the northwest and that the invasion force of tankers and transports and so forth would be coming in from the Carolines and the Marshalls.* So following the doctrine in those days, I stationed all the submarines to the northwest of Midway. Well, we showed it to Nimitz and Nimitz, it was my impression, wouldn't quite believe that what he was getting was the straight dope, so he made me put some submarines to the southwest of Midway and a few more to the northwest of Oahu. I think we had four northwest of Oahu, three somewhere southeast of Midway.

Q: So he was hedging his bets.

Admiral Walker: He was hedging his bets, but because he hedged his bets, the only real submarine contact was in the Nautilus.

Q: She got the Soryu, I think.

---

*The "big staff" refers to people working directly for Admiral Chester Nimitz, Commander in Chief Pacific Fleet. Decrypted Japanese messages were being supplied to Commander Edwin T. Layton, Nimitz's intelligence officer, and then went to the submarine force.

Admiral Walker: That's right. She put the coup de grâce on the Soryu. Yes. And she had just been modernized. As I recall, I can't remember for sure, I think they had taken the guns off of her at that time. I don't remember, but she had got a new air-conditioning system and new torpedo data computer and new engines and everything.

Q: She was also used for minelaying.

Admiral Walker: There was another one, three of them, three big ones. There was the Narwhal, the Nautilus, and the minelayer was the Argonaut.

Q: The others had that mission also. I know the Nautilus laid mines.

Admiral Walker: Yes, but these were torpedo mines. They laid them out of torpedo tubes. But there was only one minelayer that laid regular mines, and she was no good because she was so damn noisy. The Argonaut made a real big racket. She and the Nautilus, as I remember, went on the Makin Island raid, Jimmy Roosevelt and I planned the Makin Island raid.* Jimmy that time was exec to Colonel Carlson, of Carlson's Raiders, and I was

---

*Major James Roosevelt, USMCR, son of President Franklin D. Roosevelt.

Walker #1 - 178

operations officer for ComSubPac, and we planned the Makin Island raid together.*

Q: Well, tell me more. Where and when did you do this?

Admiral Walker: Well, that was in the spring of '42. I don't remember the exact date now, but in the spring of '42.

Q: In Hawaii?

Admiral Walker: Yes.

Q: And it was planned as a diversion for the Guadalcanal operation.

Admiral Walker: As I remember, at that time, we had no dope about being a diversion from Guadalcanal. It was just to annoy the Japs up there in that part where they'd never been annoyed before to show that they couldn't sit in places on their dead butts and do nothing. I don't recall any coordination with

---

*Lieutenant Colonel Evans F. Carlson, USMC, commanding officer, 2d Raider Battalion. On the night of 17 August 1942, less than two weeks after the American landing at Guadalcanal, two companies of Marines from Carlson's Raiders went ashore on Makin in rubber boats. They had been transported to the scene by the submarines Nautilus (SS-168) and Argonaut (SM-1). The raid produced mixed results.

Walker #1 - 179

Guadalcanal at all. At least nobody talked about it to me, as I can remember.

Q: I think that was the general thing, to tell people only as much as they needed to know.

Admiral Walker: That's right. That's right.

Q: Do you remember any details of the planning with him?

Admiral Walker: No, I don't remember any of the details. It was just figuring how many men we could carry on each boat and how we'd get them ashore in the life rafts and we'd use the big 6-inch guns to bombard the shore installation. And they were going ashore without any preparation at daybreak--I can remember that--in these big rubber boats.

Q: What kind of a guy was Jimmy Roosevelt to work with?

Admiral Walker: Oh, okay. He was all right. He seemed to be fairly knowledgeable about Carlson's Raiders and what they could do and what their capabilities were of the Marines and so forth.

Q: Was there any idea that he deserved special treatment because he was the President's son?

Walker #1 - 180

Admiral Walker: Not really. No, no. He was a major at that time.

Q: Yes. Getting back to these minelaying operations, how did you pick out the areas that you wanted to concentrate on?

Admiral Walker: Well, just where we knew that the greatest concentration of shipping would be or probably would be, because we didn't know too much. We didn't have any planes scouting for us, or we didn't have anyone up in the sky there looking down telling us what was going on. We just had to sort of try and figure out from what information we could pick up from the submarines when they came back when they gave us their patrol reports, where the traffic was, and probably--of course, we studied the maps to get the depth of water and so forth in the probable areas. And, in general, there wasn't too much mining--at least before I left.

Q: That's right.

Admiral Walker: See, I was detached about the first of August, and I came back with my wife and children. Miriam was allowed to stay because I was there, and so we all came back together on a United Fruit boat.

Q: How important were the patrol reports in planning future operations?

Admiral Walker: They were quite important. We went over them very carefully. Very carefully.

Q: And I imagine these also gave you a tip-off on who the better skippers were.

Admiral Walker: Oh, sure. And some were better writers than others. You weren't always sure which was what.

Q: How much did you rely on the input from the squadron commanders? I know Babe Brown was important out there at a point during the war.*

Admiral Walker: Up until the time I left, we didn't--English had been squadron commander of Squadron Four before he became ComSubPac, but we had no input at all from the squadron commanders, and the squadron commanders were practically nonentities, because we handled all operations. They didn't do any operations work at all. We handled all the boats from the big staff. And the division commanders didn't do anything at

---

*Captain John H. Brown, USN, Commander Submarine Squadron Four.

that time except routine administrative work, looked after getting supplies for their boats and things like that. But neither the division nor squadron commanders were in the operational chain of command at all.

Q: Well, they did have a say in who got picked as skippers, didn't they?

Admiral Walker: I don't recall too much of that. They may have. They may have been talking to the boss and I didn't know anything about it. As for going through me, no.

Q: What changes, if any, came about when Admiral Withers was relieved by Admiral English?

Admiral Walker: Well, it was like a new broom, you know. Admiral English was very meticulous, especially about writing letters. I know the first couple I wrote, he jumped on me. Whenever you wrote for Admiral English, you had to write a general paragraph first, then you had to go one, two, three, four, five, six, sign off. You didn't do that with Withers necessarily, but that's the only way you could write a letter for English and get it by him.

Q: I guess it's your job to adapt to the boss.

Admiral Walker: That's for sure.

Q: Was he more in keeping with Admiral Nimitz than Admiral Withers had been?

Admiral Walker: I think so, yes. I have a feeling with Withers and Nimitz weren't too simpatico. By that I mean, I don't think Nimitz thought Withers was the greatest guy in the world. I think maybe he thought he was a little bit too complacent. That's the feeling I had. I didn't know, of course.

Q: Had you had any dealing with the staff before Admiral Nimitz came in, that is, with Admiral Kimmel's staff?

Admiral Walker: No. I had no dealings at all with Admiral Kimmel's staff.

Q: When Nimitz then came in, how much control did he exert over submarine operations?

Admiral Walker: Practically none. The only time I remember him getting into it at all is when we set up the Midway operation. Otherwise, I don't remember him monitoring our operations. He had nothing to do with how we picked the operating areas around Japan or the Carolines, the Marshall islands. Now he may have

Walker #1 - 184

told English how to do some of those things, but none of his staff ever in any way talked to me about that. I'd get word from the chief of staff if he wanted some changes in submarine operations. Now, whether he made them up in his own mind or Withers or English was telling him, or Nimitz was telling him, I don't know. But as far as the operation of the submarines was concerned, picking out the going and coming and the operating areas and the type of weapons they'd carry, like mines and torpedoes and so forth, all my directions came from the chief of staff.

Q: Was there a staff intelligence officer that you worked with at all?

Admiral Walker: We didn't have one.

Q: Sounds as if there was certainly a job there for one.

Admiral Walker: Yes. No, we didn't have one.

Q: So you think again that the admiral was the conduit to these crypto people?

Admiral Walker: Yes, the admiral and the chief of staff.

Q: Did you have any dealings with Jasper Holmes, who was also working with them?*

Admiral Walker: I knew he was working on decoding of some kind, but I didn't know what kind of dope he was getting. I knew he was in the decoding group over in the navy yard. I knew all about that. I knew one of the boys over there in decoding, was a man in '26, Ham Wright, who'd been in PG school with me and was an ordnance PG.**

Q: Holmes was more of a liaison man. He was not one of the codebreakers, but he was the guy who dealt with, say, SubPac and the other commands.

Admiral Walker: Yes. As I say, I knew he was over there and that's the kind of work he was doing, but as to getting the Ultra, I never had--the only time I had any inkling of that was in about February when the Gudgeon was on her way back from patrol, and we were told that a Jap submarine would be at a certain latitude and longitude at an approximate time, and we sent out a message to Joe Grenfell to attack it and he got it,

---
*Lieutenant Wilfred J. Holmes, USN(Ret.). Holmes's recollections of the period are contained in his book Double-Edged Secrets, published by the Naval Institute Press, 1979.
**Lieutenant Commander Wesley A. Wright, USN.

Walker #1 - 186

and fortunately the torpedo worked.* But otherwise than that, I didn't get very much.

Q: One very famous story about Ultra is Captain Cromwell going down with the submarine rather than revealing classified information.**

Admiral Walker: You know, Cromwell was one of the nicest guys I ever knew, but he was the scariest guy I ever knew.

Q: Scary in what sense?

Admiral Walker: He was always worried about some plane coming in to attack. And the night that the Jap planes came in and attacked Oahu in about March of '42, old John was having a fit about it. I was down in the office on duty, and my office was

---

*On 27 January 1942, the USS Gudgeon (SS-211), commanded by Lieutenant Commander Elton W. Grenfell, USN, sank the Japanese submarine I-173 on the basis of radio intercept information. She was the first major Japanese combatant sunk in World War II and the first sunk on the basis of radio intelligence. For details, see Clay Blair, Jr., Silent Victory: The U.S. Submarine War Against Japan (Philadelphia: J.B. Lippincott Company, 1975), pages 117-118.

**Captain John P. Cromwell, USN, Commander Submarine Division 43, was embarked in the USS Sculpin (SS-191) on 18 November 1943 when she lost a gun duel with the Japanese destroyer Yamagumo. After the skipper had been killed, the senior surviving officer ordered the boat scuttled. Captain Cromwell elected to go down with the submarine rather than reveal what he knew about Ultra and upcoming operations. He was awarded a posthumous Medal of Honor.

right next to the admiral's, and I was there most of the night. But John was always jittery. He was one of the nicest guys I ever knew.

Q: What job did he have that gave him this fund of knowledge that was worth dying for?

Admiral Walker: He was a division commander in command of a wolf pack, and he had been well-briefed before the wolf pack went out about what was going on and where all the ships in the American Navy were, the destroyers and the other ships. So he should have had a pretty good picture at the time, and apparently rather than run the risk of being tortured by the Japs, he decided to go down. Somewhat like Gilmore he decided to go down.* I sometimes wonder if I'd have had the guts to do those things. I was never tested that way.

Q: You'd never know 'til you got there.

Admiral Walker: That's right. It's too late now.

---

*On 7 February 1943, Lieutenant Commander Howard W. Gilmore, USN, was in command of the USS Growler (SS-215) when she rammed a Japanese gunboat and suffered a heavy machine gun attack. Gilmore ordered his executive officer to "Take her down," thus sacrificing his own life in order to ensure the safety of the submarine and the remainder of her crew. He was posthumously awarded the Medal of Honor.

Walker #2 - 188

Interview Number 2 with Rear Admiral Edward K. Walker,
U.S. Navy (Retired)

Place: Admiral Walker's home, Glen Rock, New Jersey

Date: Wednesday, 12 September 1984

Subject: Biography

Interviewer: Paul Stillwell

Q: Admiral, last night when we broke off, we were talking about your service on the SubPac staff.* Did you have an optimistic feeling about the progress of the war as that year 1942 went forward?

Admiral Walker: Yes, especially after the Battle of Midway. I never had a discouraged feeling. I always felt that we'd make it in the end. We were a little slow starting because of various conditions, but I never was pessimistic about the outcome.

Q: Could you discuss the controversy between Admiral English and the submarine skippers who were posted out near Midway?** He thought they weren't aggressive enough, and they didn't think his disposition of forces gave them sufficient opportunity.

---

*SubPac--Submarine Force, Pacific Fleet.
**Rear Admiral Robert H. English, USN, Commander Submarine Force Pacific Fleet.

Admiral Walker: I don't remember too many complaints from the submarine skippers concerning the disposition of the submarines around Midway. The operation areas of the submarines were given to me by the chief of staff. I don't know whether they were his idea or whether he had instructions from above.

Q: You were still being plagued at that time by those torpedo failures. What efforts were you making to counteract that?

Admiral Walker: We really weren't sure of the cause of the torpedo failures. We went into special testing of the magnetic exploders before we put them in torpedoes, to try to be sure that they were in good condition. And also, about that time, the spring of '42, we found that the torpedoes were running deeper than they were supposed to, and corrections were made so that the torpedoes would run more nearly at the depth to which they were set. That's about it. We didn't realize there was any trouble with the exploder as far as the mechanical exploder was concerned, not until after the time I left.

Q: Were there any special briefings or training given the individual skippers and crews on what to do if they were taken prisoner?

Admiral Walker: No.

Walker #2 - 190

Q: What was the presumption at that time for behavior on the part of POWs in general—just no cooperation at all?

Admiral Walker: The only information or only instructions we had at all were what we gave if you were taken prisoner, you just do in accordance with the international convention—give your name, rank, and serial number—and that was it, period. That's the instructions you got.

Q: How much cooperation and exchange was there between SubPac as a type command and some of the other commands such as the destroyer force, carriers, and what have you?

Admiral Walker: After the war started, practically none. There was coordination before the war in the times and areas for practice and all that sort of thing, what the practices were going to be that coming week, and all that. That was all ironed out, generally, Saturday morning before the coming week so we could work up our schedules together. But after the war began, there was really no cooperation at all. I mean, we just didn't talk with them at all, except once in a while to get destroyer escorts to take our submarines in and out of the Pearl area so that they wouldn't be attacked by the Navy air or the Army air.

Q: Did you work with the destroyers to provide some training services for your submarines when they would practice before they went out?

Admiral Walker: No. As I recall, we weren't doing any practicing at all. The submarine skippers, when they were in port, would take practice on the attack teacher, but that's all. The submarines didn't go out and have torpedo practices at all after the war started.

Q: What was the priority of targets once the war got under way for a submarine skipper?

Admiral Walker: Well, when we started, battleships, heavy cruisers, destroyers, tankers. After we started unrestricted warfare, the bigger merchant ships and tankers were prime targets.

Q: When a submarine came upon a convoy, was the idea to go for the escorts first or the merchant ships first?

Admiral Walker: The idea was to avoid the escorts and go for the merchant ships.

Q: And then go for the escorts if they went for the submarine?

Admiral Walker: That's right.

Q: How much did you as the operations officer get into tactics with the individual submarines?

Admiral Walker: None at all.

Q: That was left to the skippers?

Admiral Walker: That is correct. And any training or discussion between the skippers and their division commanders and so forth, the squadron commanders, but we didn't get into that at all. We just scheduled them all where they went and their operation areas and all that sort of thing. But the individual training of the boats, we didn't get into at all.

Q: Are there any skippers that you particularly remember from your dealings with them?

Admiral Walker: John Murphy, a good friend of mine in the Tambor, and Joe Grenfell, whom I knew very well, and he had been with me in the Florida.* Let's see. There are lots of others.

---

*Lieutenant Commander John W. Murphy, Jr., USN, was first commanding officer of the USS Tambor (SS-198); Lieutenant Commander Elton W. Grenfell, USN, was the first commanding officer of the USS Gudgeon (SS-211).

Some of my best friends that I knew quite well were all out with the Asiatic Fleet in Fremantle.

Q: Somebody like Sam Dealey liked to try the down-the-throat shot.* Was that encouraged or discouraged?

Admiral Walker: I was the originator of that shot.

Q: Oh, were you?

Admiral Walker: Yes, I was the originator of that shot, and that was really after I left and took command of the destroyer Mayrant. I wrote a letter to Ed Swinburne, the flag secretary, strongly recommending that it be tried.** Of course, this was on the basis that the magnetic exploder was working, and the idea being that if the submarine showed a periscope and a destroyer started to chase it, then you'd fire right down the throat at it with the stern tube. And if the destroyer started to turn at all to avoid the torpedo she'd yaw and make a bigger target. And

---

*Commander Samuel D. Dealey, USN, was commanding officer when the USS Harder (SS-257) went into commission on 2 December 1942. If the destroyer turned either way while chasing the submarine, she would theoretically get a torpedo in the side. Dealey won the Medal of Honor for his exploits in the Harder. He and the submarine were lost on 24 August 1944.
**A copy of Swinburne's response to Walker's letter is included as an appendix to this volume. It discusses early attempts at use of the tactic by Lieutenant Commander Dudley W. "Mush" Morton, USN, while in command of the USS Wahoo (SS-238).

with the magnetic, it couldn't miss. And I strongly recommended that they try it. Well, they had a couple unfortunate experiences. No submarine actually got hit, but the torpedoes didn't go off. I think they didn't use it too much after '44. But they used it quite a bit in '43.

Q: Could you talk about the process in which your relief came about?

Admiral Walker: The admiral said that nobody had to stay more than two years. I had gone out in 1940, in June, so by June of '42, I would have had two years on the staff. So in the spring of '42, around April or May, I asked to command a submarine, and they said, "No, you're too old and you're too senior." They didn't want anybody over 35.

They figured the older ones weren't aggressive enough, and I was older than that and quite a bit senior, so I said, "Okay, how about a division?"

They said, "No, we're not giving divisions to anybody unless they're a commander." Well, they had run up the new promotion list that April or May, but they went down through '24 and stopped. So '25, we were still lieutenant commanders, and '24 were commanders.

So that's when I requested command of a destroyer. The first orders that came out were as gunnery officer of a carrier. Well,

I didn't want that. I wanted command. So I wrote to my friend, Bill Kitts, who'd been my boss in the fire control section of the bureau, to see if he could arrange with Bill Fechteler, who was then the detail officer, to get me a destroyer.* And sure enough, orders came back for me to command the Mayrant.

When it came time for me to be relieved, I was asked to make a recommendation for my relief, and I recommended that John Murphy, the commanding officer of the Tambor and a classmate of mine, a real smart man, relieve me. Admiral English vetoed that on the basis that they were a little unhappy with John Murphy, because at the Battle of Midway on the morning following the battle, he had reported sighting three Japanese ships in the dim light--I don't think he definitely identified them.** I can't remember for sure on that point. But he failed to report the course and speed, and I think one of the reasons was that they were maneuvering and changing course and speed quite a bit when he saw them. But anyway, the admiral was unhappy about that, so then I recommended that Dick Voge be brought up from the Southwest Pacific to become operations officer.*** He had lost

---
*Commander Willard A. Kitts III, USN. Captain William M. Fechteler, USN, who was then in the Bureau of Personnel. As an admiral, Fechteler served as Chief of Naval Operations from 1951 to 1953.
**Rear Admiral Robert H. English, USN, Commander Submarine Force Pacific Fleet.
***Commander Richard G. Voge, USN, who wound up serving as SubPac operations officer during much of the war and making a substantial contribution to the success of U.S. submarines against the Japanese. His submarine, the USS Sailfish (SS-192), had previously been the ill-fated Squalus.

his command at the bombing of Cavite, but he'd been given another command, the <u>Sailfish</u>, which I think he made one or two patrols in.

John Murphy's experience is an illustration of how one thing can affect your career in the Navy. I am sure John would have made admiral but for the ambiguous message he sent out the morning after the Battle of Midway. Because of that, he was turned down as my relief as operations officer of ComSubPac. If he had relieved me, he would have been operations officer for Admiral Lockwood instead of Dick Voge and would probably have written the book <u>Submarine Operations in World War II</u>.

When my class was getting command of S-boats in 1934 and 1935, most of us had previous submarine experience of three to five years. Dick Voge took command of the <u>S-18</u> at the same time I took command of the <u>S-21</u>. He had only one year's experience in submarines before getting command, and some people resented it. Shortly after he took command, he made a dive, and the after battery hatch had not been properly secured, and the boat received rather severe flooding in the after battery compartment.

Q: You mentioned Admiral English. Was he still alive at the point when you left the staff?

Admiral Walker: Yes, he was. It was just a week or two after I left that he made the plane trip to California for a conference and bumped into a mountain in the fog.

Q: Is it likely you would have been along on that trip if you had still been on the staff?

Admiral Walker: I don't think so. The only two people on the staff on that trip was John Crane, the engineer, and Reilly Coll, the torpedo and gunnery officer.* The admiral took them along because they'd been in Pearl for six or eight months or more and hadn't seen their families in all that time, so this was just an opportunity for them to see their families for a few days.

Q: And your family had been out there, so you certainly had seen them.

Admiral Walker: I wouldn't have been aboard, no.

Q: Well, you've already described how you came to get command of the Mayrant. Why don't you then tell how it was when you

---

　　*On 21 January 1943, a Pan American Clipper carrying 19 people, including crew members, crashed into the side of a cliff near Boonville, California, and all on board were killed, including Admiral English, Commander John J. Crane, USN, and Lieutenant Commander John Owen Reilly Coll, USN. For further details, see Clay Blair Jr., Silent Victory: The U.S. Submarine War Against Japan (Philadelphia: J.B. Lippincott Company, 1975), pages 365-366.
　A letter from Lieutenant Commander Edwin R. Swinburne, found in the appendix to this volume, provides more details on the crash.

reported aboard.

Admiral Walker: Okay. When I left Pearl Harbor, I went to San Diego first, and there went to the antisubmarine school for a couple of weeks. And then my family and I went across the country by train and landed in Norfolk. The Mayrant was out on maneuvers and training somewhere in the Chesapeake, I forget where. And I was taken out to her and went aboard one day and talked with the commanding officer and relieved him the next morning, and there I was commanding officer of the Mayrant. As I say, when I stepped aboard the Mayrant, that was my first day's duty in a destroyer. I was commanding officer.

Q: Sounds as if you could have used a bit more turnover than you had.

Admiral Walker: Right. I really could have, but I didn't get it.

Q: How much did your submarine experience benefit you in shiphandling with a destroyer?

Admiral Walker: Oh, it was wonderful. I had no problems whatsoever with shiphandling. The only problem I had in the destroyer, as I said, was surface maneuvering, which I'd never grown up with in submarines, tactical maneuvering. And I had to keep reading the book all the time.

Q: How long did that take you to catch on?

Admiral Walker: Well, during the war, not very long because there wasn't much of that sort of thing, because we were mainly convoy escorts. The first operation I went on was the invasion of North Africa, and we went shortly after I took command. We went from Norfolk to Portland, Maine, to join up with the task group that we were with. I was in DesRon Eight. The DesRon commander was D.P. Moon, "Dipper" Moon.* He was an ordnance PG, and he was a very meticulous sort of guy. As a matter of fact, later he shot himself when he had command of portions of the invasion of Southern Europe.** And I'll never forget, after we left Portland, we were just assigned as a screen to the main body of the group we were with, which consisted of the Massachusetts, Wichita, and another heavy cruiser, Tuscaloosa, and the five destroyers of DesRon Eight at that time. And I'll never forget, just as soon as it would come daylight every morning, Moon's light on the bridge would start to go and he'd

---

*Captain Don P. Moon, USN, Commander Destroyer Squadron Eight.
**For details on the events leading to Moon's death, see Samuel Eliot Morison, The Inversion of France and Germany: 1944-1945, Volume XI of History of United States Naval Operations in World War II (Boston: Little, Brown and Company, 1957), pages 241-242.

Walker #2 - 200

start asking me a whole bunch of questions about what was I doing about this, what I was doing about that, what I was doing. I never had any time to read the operations orders; I spent all my time answering foolish questions.

Q: So you think he was too thorough?

Admiral Walker: Oh, he was a pain in the neck, terrible. Well, there's an anecdote, long before the war when he had a destroyer division, they were out maneuvering and practicing, and they would simulate this and simulate that and simulate the other thing. And so in one maneuver, one of the ships made a very poor performance, so Moon sent a dispatch immediately, "Who's the officer of the deck?"

And they sent back, "We are simulating Ensign So-and-so, who is now in torpedo school."

Q: Was most of the communication visual during that transit?

Admiral Walker: It was all visual.

Q: Did you avoid radio use?

Admiral Walker: That's right, yes. And we didn't have any submarine scares at all on the way over. Of course, we didn't know what was going to happen, what the French were going to do. And the operation order said if the French resisted, then we would get the signal, "Play ball." So sure enough, just as we were off of Casablanca that morning, about 7:00 o'clock in the morning, we got the signal, "Play ball," and we got some air attacks from the French. During that day we made about, as I recall it, three runs past the forts there at Casablanca. And there's a good story connected with that. In making these runs, I was the leading destroyer on the inboard side. There were five of us screening, one dead ahead, one on each bow, one on each beam. And I was having a little bit of a problem with my blowers that morning. I'd smoke a little once in a while because we were steaming anywhere from 33 to 35 knots, especially when I was trying to get up ahead of the Massachusetts. She was doing close to 30 knots herself during this period. The French fort, El Hank, thought that they had hit me, so they all concentrated on me. So everywhere I looked was a colored splash coming up all around, so what did we do, we'd wait for a salvo to land and then we'd chase the salvo.* And then they'd make the correction and we weren't there anymore. That day I had a messenger who was a young Irish lad from South Boston. His name was Scanlon. During the day, every time there would be a lull after we'd finish a run and make a turn to come back for another run, I'd miss him. So

---

*Projectiles contained dyes of various colors so that different batteries would know which shells were landing closest to the target.

at the end of the day, I said, "Scanlon, what happened to you? Every time there was a lull in the proceedings and we were making a turn and coming back to start all over, you were gone. What happened?"

"Well," he said, "captain, it was like this. Every time there was a lull, I ran as fast as I could to my abandon ship station. Each time I timed myself, and then I said, 'Scanlon, you've got to do better next time.'" That's a true story.

Q: That was your first real test under fire. How did you react to it?

Admiral Walker: It's a sort of strange feeling. That's all I can say. To know that you personally were being shot at and everybody was concentrating on you. Fortunately, we didn't get hit.

Q: Was there the natural fear and apprehension one might expect in that situation?

Admiral Walker: Oh, there's always some, yes. Yep.

Q: How good were the junior officers assigned to that ship?

Admiral Walker: At that time, I only had one Naval Academy

officer, that was the executive officer, Edes Talman.* My gunnery officer was Franklin D. Roosevelt, Jr.** My torpedo officer was Bob Watson, who had been Frank's roommate at Harvard and later became a dean and also director of athletics at Harvard University.*** And then the rest were—well, I'm taking it back. I had two ensigns that were Naval Academy graduates. Larry Savadkin was my engineer officer; he was later in submarines.****

Q: Sounds like you had a fair amount of talent on board.

Admiral Walker: Yes, I did. Yes. Franklin Roosevelt was a crackerjack naval officer. He was excellent. He was one of the few reserve officers I had with me. Bob Watson was the same, too. I could go to sleep at night peacefully, knowing that if he got into trouble, he either could get out of it or know enough to know that he couldn't and give me a call. My biggest trouble was they didn't want to wake me up. They'd get the ship in trouble that was difficult to get it out of, because they'd wait too long to call me. But Frank either could handle the situation or he knew enough to call you. And he was a good gunnery officer. He was gunnery officer at the invasion of Casablanca.

---
*Lieutenant Benjamin L.E. Talman, USN.
**Lieutenant Franklin D. Roosevelt, Jr., USNR, later executive officer.
***Lieutenant Robert B. Watson, USNR.
****Lieutenant Lawrence Savadkin, USN.

Then we came back from that and went back on another convoy run to Casablanca in December, and I was over there over Christmas. And while we were there, one day the aide to the admiral ashore came out to the ship, and he said, "I want to take Lieutenant Roosevelt ashore with me. The admiral will assure you that he will get Roosevelt back to you at least 12 hours before you depart back to the States." So I said okay. So he went and saw Frank, and Frank went and got in his clothes. Before he left, Frank came up on the bridge.

I said, "For God's sake, Frank, what's going on?"

"Oh," he said, "the old man's here." Sure enough, they got him back to me about a day before we left to return home. And then we came back to the States.*

While we were in Casablanca, over the Christmas period or shortly thereafter, we got ordered to go south to the port of Safi, which is about 150, 200 miles south of Casablanca, to act as antiaircraft protection for the port. So when I got in, I went ashore and called on the Navy captain of the port, who was a man out of '21. I forget his name. I said, "Is there anybody else around here I should call on while I'm here?"

"Well," he said, "there's a French naval captain here and there's a local pasha. Don't bother. You don't need to."

Well, I thought, "Maybe I don't need to, but I think I will."

---

*From 14 to 23 January 1943, President Roosevelt, Prime Minister Winston Churchill, and the Combined Chiefs of Staff met at Casablanca to plan Allied strategy for the conduct of the war.

So I went over to call on the naval captain. The next day I got a note saying that he would be very happy if I could come for dinner that night, and if Lieutenant Roosevelt wasn't going to be busy, he hoped I would bring Lieutenant Roosevelt with me. So I said, "Frank, you want to go out to this naval captain's for dinner?"

He said, "Sure." So we went over and had a delightful dinner.

Well, the next morning, I got an urgent call from the captain of the port. He says, "You've got to help me out. We're in trouble."

I said, "What's the matter?"

"Well," he says, "it seems like Mrs. Captain called up Mrs. Governor [the French governor] and said, 'I had the son of the President of the United States for dinner last night, Honey. How are you doing?'"

So he said, "Will you please take Roosevelt with you and go call on the French governor and also while you're about it, call on the local pasha?"

So it happened also that the local pasha was the son of the Grand Vizier of Morocco, which is the same as a prime minister. So Frank and I, we went over and called on the governor and he was pleased to see us and asked us for dinner two or three days later. Then we went over and called on the native pasha. He was very pleasant and said that he wanted us to have dinner. But it took at least two days to prepare the dinner and we would have to wait for two more days, and he certainly hoped we would be there then. Unfortunately, we got orders to leave the next morning, so I missed that pasha's dinner. It's always been the regret of my life that I missed that pasha's dinner, because I think it would have been most interesting.

Q: Especially if it took two days to fix.

Admiral Walker: You can see the kinds of problems that Roosevelt would cause at times.

Q: Well, it sounds like they weren't entirely unpleasant problems.

Admiral Walker: Oh, no, they weren't.

Q: You had met his brother earlier for planning the Makin raid. Did you draw any comparisons between the two?

Admiral Walker: Yes, I think Frank was a little more outgoing than Jimmy was. Also I'd met his brother John while I was in San Diego going to school. He was a young supply officer at the time. I had met John out at San Diego and used to ride back and forth with him every morning on the boat from San Diego to North

Island.

Q: So you ran right through the family.

Walker: I sure did.

Q: Did politics ever come up as a wardroom discussion?

Admiral Walker: No. No.

Q: Was it a pretty convivial wardroom?

Admiral Walker: Very. Yes, it was. Yes.

Q: That's one advantage that the small ship has, the captain can eat with his officers.

Admiral Walker: That's true. Of course, it's a little different than in a large ship. At night I used to have to wear red goggles for dinner, so I'd be all set for night vision in case there was a submarine attack against the convoy. And we did have a couple. We lost a couple of ships on one of the convoys we were taking over. The second convoy went over around December; we ran into a real bad storm coming out of New York and the convoy was all broken up and scattered. We finally collected them and got them all back together again, and it was so rough, we didn't lose any ships. I mean, the submarines were just keeping out of the weather, so it wasn't bothering us, it was so bad.

Q: How capable was that class as far as ASW was concerned?*

Admiral Walker: As capable as any destroyer of the time. They had the latest equipment that was available, and when I first went aboard, we only had the SC search radar, you know, up at the top of the mast, and also we had the fire control radar. Later, we got the SG search radar. We had that, I remember, for the battle at Casablanca. That was really the first operation I was on.

Q: Did you do any shooting at Casablanca?

Admiral Walker: Oh, yes, we were shooting all the time at the forts. The Massachusetts, the two heavy cruisers were shooting, and all the destroyers on the side toward the beach, which I was, were also shooting. And also we did some antiaircraft shooting.

Q: You got to do a little of everything.

---

*ASW--antisubmarine warfare.

Admiral Walker: That's right.

Q: Where did you get the target assignments for shore bombardment?

Admiral Walker: As I remember, we shot at where the flashes were coming from ashore. We didn't get any specific assignment, as I recall.

Q: Had your crew had any specific training in shore bombardment?

Admiral Walker: I don't know. Not while I was aboard.

Q: So it was, I guess, just a direct fire control problem. You see a flash and aim for it.

Admiral Walker: That's right.

Q: Was there any hesitance or reluctance on the part of the crew in having you come aboard with no destroyer experience, or did they show anything like that?

Admiral Walker: I don't know whether they even knew that. Of course, the officers did, but I doubt that the crew did. And to the best of my knowledge, no.

Walker #2 - 210

Q: Did you feel that there was an effort on their part to help you get this in a hurry since you didn't have that kind of experience? Did they rally around you?

Admiral Walker: Yes, but I don't think for that reason. They were a little bit unhappy with the previous skipper, and they seemed to be happy that I was there.

Q: What was the basis for their unhappiness with him?

Admiral Walker: I don't know, really. He was a little bit persnickety. I remember one of the officers telling me later on they were put out with him, so they used to make a habit of body checking him when they got an opportunity on the bridge, would go near him and accidentally body check him.*

Q: So you were welcome just because you were somebody else.

Admiral Walker: I think so. No, and I never noticed that there was any feeling whatsoever. As I say, I doubt that the crew knew that I hadn't had previous destroyer experience.

Q: Did you catch on fairly quickly, would you say?

---

*A body check in hockey is a deliberate collision with a player on the opposing team. The previous commanding officer of the *Mayrant* was Commander Edwin A. Taylor, USN.

Admiral Walker: Oh, yes. I couldn't see any difference at all. As I say, the only problem I had, I wasn't completely conversant with destroyer tactics, tactical operation, but during the period of the war, this didn't come up at all. So it really made little difference, because all we were doing was screening. We weren't operating as a tactical group attacking another battle line or anything like that.

Q: I've heard that one difficulty that submarine skippers have in making a transition to surface ships is that in submarines they're used to running a one-man show, whereas you have to delegate more in a surface ship. You can't be running the thing 24 hours a day. Were you able to do that?

Admiral Walker: I never noticed any problem at all. I'm the best delegator in the world.

Q: More a matter of personality than having been in submarines.

Admiral Walker: Yes. That's right.

Q: How much time did you spend on the bridge under way?

Admiral Walker: Well, during the war, I spent most of the day and, when things were rough like in a storm, I just slept in my chair on the bridge at night.

Q: Did you have a sea cabin?

Admiral Walker: I had a sea cabin, but it had two sound stacks in it, so it was awful noisy.* It wasn't much good, really. I'd rather sleep in my chair on the bridge wrapped in a blanket than go down and bunk in that sea cabin, which was one level down below under the bridge. Why they put all those sound stacks in there, I don't know, except they didn't have any other place to put them.

Q: What were the ship's operations after that?

Admiral Walker: We came back from North Africa some time after the first of the year, and then we went into overhaul in the New York Navy Yard. It came time for us to leave the New York Navy Yard and get ready to join the group and take a convoy over for the invasion of Sicily. And the morning we were supposed to leave, we were supposed to leave at 8:00 o'clock, and it got to be about 7:30 or a quarter to 8:00, and no Roosevelt. So I asked the officer of the deck how come, and he said, "Roosevelt came

---

*The assembled electronic components of sonar gear are referred to as the "sound stack" or "sonar stack." The ship was designed before the development of sonar, so the equipment had to be retrofitted wherever there was room--in this case, the captain's sea cabin.

aboard about 11:00 o'clock last night. He got up early this morning, at 6:00 o'clock and left the ship, and I haven't seen him since."

Well, I was sort of on the spot. What do I do now? So I notified the commandant of the yard that Lieutenant Roosevelt was missing, and also sent a dispatch to the Navy Department in Washington that Roosevelt was missing. We were just about five minutes of 8:00. They sent the Marines searching for him, and they found Frank in a telephone booth sound asleep. What had happened--he'd got up and gone to this telephone booth to call his mother to tell her he was leaving the next day, and fallen asleep in the telephone booth. But we finally got him aboard just before we sailed.*

Q: Was he still the gunnery officer, or had he become exec by then?

Admiral Walker: He had become exec by then, because he was exec for the invasion of Sicily, and we took a large convoy over to Oran. Then we operated out of Mers-el-Kebir, which is the French naval port right there. And for two or three months there, we were just running convoys along the North African coast from Oran

---

*The Mayrant left the New York Navy Yard in Brooklyn on 3 March 1943 and went to an anchorage off Sandy Hook, New Jersey. On 5 March, the ship joined Task Force 33 in convoy to Casablanca.

to points east.

I remember one incident. The Army was around then and they had sent over a bunch of Army nurses. Some of our officers met them, so we had three or four over for dinner one night. Well, the next morning, I was tied up alongside the squadron flagship. Charlie Wellborn was squadron commander at that time.* Of course, the bridges were almost side by side. And Wellborn said, "I understand you had women aboard for dinner last night. Don't you know that the commander in chief, Admiral Cunningham, said there will be no women aboard ship?"**

I said, "Yes, I understand that, but Commodore, we didn't have women aboard; we had Army officers." So that was the end of the episode.

Q: You couldn't tell the difference.

What are your recollections of Admiral Wellborn? I have met him on several occasions.

Admiral Walker: He was a great guy. I enjoyed working under him very much.

---

*Captain Charles Wellborn, Jr., USN, Commander Destroyer Squadron Eight. His flagship was the USS _Wainwright_ (DD-419). Wellborn eventually reached the rank of vice admiral; his oral history is in the Naval Institute collection.
**Admiral of the Fleet Sir Andrew B. Cunningham, Royal Navy, Commander in Chief Mediterranean. Later in 1943, Cunningham was elevated to the post of First Sea Lord.

Q: How would you contrast him with Commodore Moon?

Admiral Walker: No comparison. He expected the people to do their job and would be very happy to help out or give any assistance he could, but he wasn't the type to harass you continuously like Moon was.

Q: He's a very quiet, low-key guy.

Admiral Walker: Yes, he is. Yes, he's a great guy. I enjoyed him very much.

Q: And he knows his business.

Admiral Walker: He does. Yes. Of course, he had a reputation as he was going up of being a member of the society of aides.* It seemed like he was always an aide to some admiral as he was a young officer growing up, rather than actually doing any operations himself, but he turned out to be an excellent squadron commander.

Q: How was he as far as maneuvering the ships? Did you have occasion to see that?

---

*At the beginning of World War II, while he was in the rank of commander, Wellborn had been aide to the Chief of Naval Operations, Admiral Harold R. Stark, USN.

Admiral Walker: No. No, we didn't do any at all. It was all just convoy work, and a lot of it was just one or two of the ships of the squadron at a time taking a convoy along the north coast of Africa.

Q: Did you operate in company with him at all at sea?

Admiral Walker: Only on the convoy going over to Europe.

Q: Then is it just a matter that you get assigned to station and that's it?

Admiral Walker: That's it. That's right. On the invasion of Sicily, we were one of the last groups to leave Oran, and we were escorting a group of LSTs, and we got there just about as the battle was starting after the invasion.* We were there after the invasion, mostly as antiaircraft protection for the invasion fleet. And we did some of it. We were right off the port of Licata in southern Sicily. I can't remember the name of it. It was the main invasion port where the Americans went in. And after about two or three days of that, we were ordered to the north coast of Sicily off Palermo, because the Army had cut across the island and were over there in the area of Palermo, and

---

*LSTs--tank landing ships, which were oceangoing amphibious landing vessels capable of going up onto the beach and dropping a bow ramp for unloading directly onto the shore.

they thought maybe the Italians or Germans would come down and bother them. So we were there as sea protection. The second morning there, our division or squadron was attacked by two or three groups of Junker Ju-88 bombers. And we shot down one or two before we were hit. But then another group came in, and we didn't catch them quite quick enough, and this one plane dropped a stick of bombs over us, and this bomb slid down my port side right at the junction between the after fire room and the forward engine room.* It blew a big hole in the side of the ship and also blew a hole in the bulkhead between the forward and after engine room and the forward and after fire room. So the whole central part of the ship was flooded, and we settled down until we had about a foot freeboard on one side and about half an inch or half a foot on the other, not much more. And we threw over as much heavy stuff as we could on topside. We almost got one torpedo launcher over the side, but we didn't quite make it. They started to throw away the records, but I made them stop that. I figured we might possibly need those. We also had a couple of minesweepers over there, and they came out.** One of them came alongside and gave me power. We lost all power, of course, and our auxiliary diesel started up, but for some reason, it lost water suction and the engine froze and stopped, and we

---
*The Mayrant was hit off Palermo at 0931 on the morning of 26 July 1943.
**These two ships were the USS Skill (AM-115) and the USS Strive (AM-117).

didn't have any power at all. So this minesweeper furnished us some power, and one was alongside, and the other was ahead, and towed us into Palermo.* We lost, I don't know, four men in the engine room and the fire room. I can't remember the exact figure, but we didn't lose too many.** We were lucky.

Q: Was that the same explosion that wounded Roosevelt?

Admiral Walker: Yes, that is correct. As I said before, the Mayrant, being an older destroyer, had big windows on the bridge rather than the small ports with heavy glass. And when the bomb hit, all the glass in the bridge windows shattered and went flying across the bridge. Also, the force of the explosion knocked all of us on the bridge off our feet, and the flying glass hit Roosevelt and gave him a fairly big cut in his hand, which had to be sewed up, which automatically gave him a purple heart.

Q: Did you have proximity fuzes in your AA projectiles then?

Admiral Walker: Yes, we did. We got them just before the

---

*Power was furnished by the Strive. For further details on this action, see Theodore Roscoe, United States Destroyer Operations in World War II (Annapolis, U.S. Naval Institute, 1953), pages 324-325.
**Roscoe's book lists the Mayrant's casualties as two men lost and 13 wounded. Among the latter was the executive officer, Lieutenant Franklin D. Roosevelt, Jr., USNR.

invasion of North Africa, as I remember it.

Q: Were those helpful in these planes you shot down?

Admiral Walker: Yes, I assume so.

Q: What did you have in the way of smaller antiaircraft?

Admiral Walker: We had several 20-millimeter and a couple of Bofors four-barrel setups, one forward and one aft, as I remember it.* These minesweepers towed us into Palermo and put us alongside a big pier there. Well, the first day we were there, on a pier over to our right, a merchant ship came in and unloaded a lot of ammunition for the Army. Well, that night the bombers came over, and it's the strangest feeling in the world when they drop those flares. You feel like you're just standing naked before the world. It's really something. Well, one of the bombers dropped a stick over this pier next to us, where all this ammunition was, which they hadn't taken away in the afternoon like they were supposed to have, and it all began exploding. We had no power, so we couldn't even shoot at the planes except with our Bofors and 20-millimeters, and it was night and you couldn't see. We had no fire control of any kind. We were doing some shooting, but it was completely ineffective. But we had to

---

*The Bofors were 40-millimeter quadruple mounts.

clear the people from the gun and get them under cover. It was just like rain almost, the shrapnel going against the side of the ship from all this exploding ammunition. And we were on the bridge when the rain first started, and one of the men on the bridge--I believe it was the quartermaster--got fairly badly wounded. Roosevelt picked him up and put him on his back and walked with him down to the sick bay. How he ever avoided getting hit, I don't know. Well, anyway, I recommended him for a Silver Star, and he got it.*

Q: It was dark in the ship? Did you have any emergency lights?

Admiral Walker: No, we didn't have any emergency lights. We were completely darkened anyway, because it was night.

Q: Did you have battle lanterns or something so that a doctor could operate in sick bay?

Admiral Walker: They had some sort of like gas electric flashlights or something. I forget the type of lighting, but there was some sort of light inside like that. We may have been getting some power from the dock at that time, a little bit, for lighting purposes down below. The ship was all dark.

---

*The air raid which set off the ammunition took place on 1 August 1943.

Q: But not enough to operate the guns.

Admiral Walker: Oh, no. We didn't have enough power to operate the 5-inch battery.

Q: Was this a long period without sleep for you during this invasion?

Admiral Walker: No, not really. We were going from south of Sicily around to the north. That was an overnight trip, and I got some sleep during the night before we were attacked the next morning.

Q: We sort of skipped over that yard period. What work was accomplished at New York while you were there?

Admiral Walker: I don't remember. Just routine overhaul and putting on some of the latest equipment. I forget now what was installed at that time. I think we got some new sound gear. I don't remember.

Q: Did you feel more confident about ASW capability when you went back out that next time?

Admiral Walker: Yes, because we had better sound equipment.

Walker #2 - 222

Q: And I suppose the crew had some good opportunities for liberty there.

Admiral Walker: Oh, yes, they had a lot of time for liberty.

Q: Did you encounter George Patton during the course of the Sicily operation?

Admiral Walker: After the attack alongside the pier, the repair people came along, and they stuffed the hole in the side of the ship with mattresses and covered it all with concrete, and then we pumped out the ship and got the bodies out and so forth. And during that period, two or three days after that, General Patton came down to say hello to Franklin Roosevelt, and there he was in all his glory with his two pearl-handled pistols.* He was really quite a guy. I had never met him before.

Q: What were your impressions of him from that meeting?

Admiral Walker: He was sort of a flamboyant type of man was the impression I got of him.

Q: Did you get the idea that he was putting on a show?

---

*Lieutenant General George S. Patton, Jr., U.S. Army, Commanding General, Seventh Army.

Walker #2 - 223

Admiral Walker: No, not really.

Q: It was just the way he was?

Admiral Walker: Just the way he was, that's correct.

Q: Did you get any insight into how the war was going ashore?

Admiral Walker: No, no, I didn't talk with him except just to greet him. After about two or three weeks, we were in good enough condition so that they towed us to Malta to be repaired. And I remember when I got off Malta, I sent, as the British would say, a signal to the admiral ashore requesting dry docking as soon as possible, because I was floating on concrete and mattresses. Shortly after we got there, we got an invitation from General Lord Gort, the commanding general of the British forces during the time of the "sitzkrieg."* He was commanding at Malta then. And so he invited Roosevelt to lunch, and, of course, he had to invite me. So we went over to his quarters and had a delicious lunch. It was quite an unusual meeting. And, of course, we all had a pink gin before lunch, and everything was very happy and pleasant.

---
*John Standish Surtees Prendergast Vereker was the 6th Viscount Gort. He was Commander in Chief of the British Expeditionary Force in France in 1939-1940, Governor of Gibraltar in 1941-1942, and Governor of Malta from 1942 to 1944.

Walker #2 - 224

Q: Was Malta still on the beleaguered list at that time?

Admiral Walker: Yes, it was, and we had several air raids while I was there, but we never got hit. And I was there about three or four weeks before my relief came. I was ordered back to the Bureau of Ordnance, so they flew me from Malta to North Africa, to Port Lyautey, and I sat around Port Lyautey for two or three days, and then got aboard a Pan American Clipper to fly back to New York. So we flew from Port Lyautey to Dakar, and at Dakar, we went in there for fueling, and we stayed overnight there, and the admiral there in command at Dakar put us all up for the night. I don't remember where, some sort of barracks or something he had. As I remember it, I think I was the senior officer. I think I stayed at the admiral's quarters, as I remember. But anyway, we had tried to get off that afternoon after we fueled, and we made three attempts, but it was so rough we couldn't get off the water. So we stayed overnight. And then the next morning, we flew to Bahia, at the very eastern part of Brazil, and stopped there overnight and fueled. Then we went from there to Trinidad, and from Trinidad to New York. I was sort of amused, in that they closed all the curtains on the windows coming into New York so that we couldn't see what we were doing. And I was trying to think, "What the hell do they think's going on? Who do they think we are, anyway, to have to close all the curtains so we can't see what's going on?" This was in the evening, 9:00 or 10:00 o'clock at night that we flew into New York.

Q: What could be the possible point of that?

Admiral Walker: That's right, what could be the possible point? By the way, on that trip from Port Lyautey to New York, one of the passengers was Ernie Pyle, the famous war correspondent.* Ernie spent most of his time sleeping in the back of the plane.

Q: Well, after what he'd been through, I couldn't blame him.

Admiral Walker: Right. He was a very interesting gentleman, very interesting.

Q: What do you recall about him?

Admiral Walker: Well, I just recall that he was a very interesting man to talk with about his experiences. I don't remember any of the details whatsoever.

Q: You had encountered another war correspondent, hadn't you? Quentin Reynolds.

---
*Ernest T. Pyle, well-known correspondent for the Scripps-Howard newspaper chain. Pyle's forte was presenting the personal side of the war through his stories about the experiences of individual servicemen.

Admiral Walker: Yes.

Q: What do you recall about that encounter?

Admiral Walker: Well, he came aboard ship in Palermo and I met him and talked with him. He was a great friend of Frank Roosevelt. Apparently he'd known him before the war. He wrote a book about his experiences.*

Q: Did you have a chance to see how well the repairs were coming at Malta before you left?

Admiral Walker: No, not much. They had hardly anything done, no.

Q: Did they have enough material there to restore the ship?

Admiral Walker: Yes, they did. They finally repaired the ship enough to get one boiler room and one engine room in operation, and my relief, Otto Scherini, brought the ship back with just one engine.** Roosevelt was still aboard and came back with her, and then he was detached and was given command of a DE and went out

---

*The epic of the Mayrant is recounted in "The Mighty May," chapter XIII of Reynold's The Curtain Rises (New York: Random House, 1944), pages 229-243.
**Lieutenant Commander Otto A. Scherini, USN.

to the Philippines.

Q: The name that sticks in my mind is the <u>Ulvert</u> <u>Moore</u> or something like that.* I can look it up, I'm sure.

Admiral Walker: I seem to remember that name, yes.

Q: Did you have any sense of disappointment in being detached from sea duty at that point?

Admiral Walker: No, not really, because I thought, "Good God, how long am I going to remain in this place?" There wasn't much to do at Malta. They had an English officers' mess hall not too far from where we were, and I used to go there to get my meals, because things were pretty crude on the <u>Mayrant</u> at that time for lack of sufficient air, water, and electricity, and so forth. The British aren't as good about the amenities in a navy yard as we are.

Q: So the crews still had to live aboard?

Admiral Walker: Yes, yes. They had to make out the best they could.

---

*Lieutenant Commander Roosevelt was the first commanding officer when the USS <u>Ulvert</u> <u>M.</u> <u>Moore</u> (DE-442) went into commission on 18 July 1944.

Q: Had you been promoted to commander by that point?

Admiral Walker: Yes, I was promoted to commander after we got back from the Christmas trip to Casablanca, so I was commander when we went over for the invasion of Sicily.

Q: How large a crew and how large a wardroom of officers did you have in that ship?

Admiral Walker: I'd say there was about, as I recall, 330 men and around ten or 12 officers. That's a close approximation.

Q: This is a good many more than you had had in your submarine command. Did you have to make any adjustments to that number of people?

Admiral Walker: No, it didn't bother me any.

Q: Did you get to know a fair number of the people on board?

Admiral Walker: Yes, I got to know, of course, all the officers who stood officer of the deck watches. I got to know Roosevelt and Bob Watson very well. The more junior ones I didn't get to know too well. Of course, Edes Tolman I knew very well, too. He was an excellent naval officer. He was my executive officer when

Walker #2 - 229

I took command of the <u>Mayrant</u>.

Q: Did you get around the ship much in inspections?

Admiral Walker: Yes, regularly. I'd go around and inspect the living quarters and engineering spaces and so forth at least once a week.

Q: How well was the administrative side of it handled? How much did you get involved in that?

Admiral Walker: I didn't get involved in that too much except to sign the papers.

Q: And from what you've said before, that was just fine with you.

Admiral Walker: That is right.

Q: Did some of the irritating administrative stuff get knocked off during the war, all the routine reports and things?

Admiral Walker: Yes, to some extent. A lot of the paperwork in peacetime had to do with the training. All that was knocked off. But the engineering reports and so forth and the log, and then

Walker #2 - 230

there was always something coming in, and they wanted reports on something or other, you know. It was just never-ending.

Q: Did you get any refresher training period at all after you came out of the yard?

Admiral Walker: No. I had a funny experience. After I came out of the yard, they let me take the ship down out of New York Harbor, but not all the way out, and come back just to see that all the engineering part of it was working okay. It was at night, coming back up the channel, the channel lights were all shrouded, so it was a little difficult to see. And on one channel buoy there was a motorboat tied up to it. I didn't know that. And the motorboat saw me coming and they started to move back. I saw this light moving, and I couldn't figure it. The next thing I knew, I was right on top of that buoy, and I swerved into it and banged up my screw, so I had to go back in the yard. They changed my screw overnight, and then I was ready to leave the next morning. That's the only time I ever hit anything as a commanding officer. That really wasn't my fault, because that guy in the motorboat was tied up to this buoy, a little white light, and just as I got near him, he got a little worried and he backed off, because I was keeping over to the right-hand side of the channel so other people could come out. Bang! And when I saw it closer, I swung a hard left and hard right and tried to kick my stern clear, but I didn't quite make it. The tide was running over that way and pushed me right into it.

Q: How capable were the people in the New York Navy Yard as far as taking care of your ship?

Admiral Walker: Excellent. Yes. They did a good job, no problems. In connection with that, while we were in the yard, we had a materiel inspection, and Captain Moon came over and inspected us. Of course, you know how things are in the yard; there were all these hoses and everything else around. This was not tip-top by any means, but everybody knows that and expects it. After the inspection was over, Moon said to me, "Walker, you're a nice fellow and a good officer, but you don't worry enough."

Q: And you wished you could say to him, "Sir, you worry too much."

Admiral Walker: Yes, I felt like saying that. I got a bang out of that: "You're a nice fellow and a good officer, but you don't worry enough." That's what he said.

Q: Well, then you got assigned to the Ford Instrument Company.

Admiral Walker: I got back, as I say, I was ordered to the Bureau of Ordnance, but when I got to Washington, Mrs. Walker came down. And I found out that instead of being ordered to the Bureau of Ordnance, I was going to be ordered to naval inspector of ordnance of the Ford Instrument Company in New York, which made me very happy because living conditions around Washington were sort of crowded at that time. I knew it would be much simpler for me to find a place to live in New York than it would be in Washington. But when I left the ship in Malta, Frank Roosevelt gave me a letter to deliver to his father, so when I got to Washington, I called up the President's secretary. What was her name?

Q: Grace Tully.

Admiral Walker: Yes. I told her who I was and that I had this letter and that Frank had asked me to deliver it to his father. Well, this was about 2:00 or 3:00 o'clock in the afternoon, and she said, "Wait a moment." Then she came back. She said, "The President would like to have you for cocktails at 5:30."

I said, "Well, Mrs. Walker's here in Washington with me."

"Oh," she said, "by all means, we'd be delighted to have Mrs. Walker come." So we got a cab from our hotel and drove up to the White House with practically no formalities at all. We got in, and we were met by the majordomo there and escorted up to the

Oval Office, and there was the President and Elliott and Harry Hopkins was there. And I think there was a relative of President Roosevelt's there, and I can't remember if Mrs. Roosevelt was there or not. Anyway, he asked me if I liked martinis, and I said, "Sure." So they brought him in the pitcher and ice and the ingredients, and he poured it in and he was the standard old-fashioned man, a two-to-one ratio man, the original formula for a martini, and they gave it to him.* You know, all the Roosevelts had the shakes. Well, he didn't have to bother to stir it at all. He just took it in hand, you know, and it got mixed up anyway. So we had cocktails, and he was asking me about Frank and some of our experiences in the Mediterranean. We were there maybe three-quarters of an hour or an hour. It was very pleasant. We enjoyed it.

Q: Did you get into any substantive discussion, or was it mostly just chitchat?

Admiral Walker: Chitchat, that's all, nothing substantive.

Q: Well, that was a pleasant change of pace.

Admiral Walker: Yes, it was. Another thing, when we were in the New York Navy Yard before the invasion of Sicily, Mrs. Roosevelt

---

*Two parts gin to one part vermouth

had myself and my wife and several of the officers over to her Washington Square apartment. She maintained an apartment in Washington Square in New York, and we were over there for cocktails one day. That was a very pleasant interlude, too. There again, there was nothing to discuss except chitchat.

Q: So where did you find a place to live when you got to New York?

Admiral Walker: We went out to Great Neck. We were looking for a place possibly to buy, but I was just a poor naval officer. I didn't have ten cents to my name. If I ever had $500 in my checking account, I thought I was rich. Well, they wouldn't even consider selling you a house with no down payment. So we had to rent a house, and we rented a house in Great Neck. And we stayed there until I left to go to sea in October of '45, and Mrs. Walker stayed on for another six months or so when she finally got put out because--I forget now. The house was sold, and she went back and stayed with her mother and dad in Newton Highlands, Massachusetts. That was very interesting. I thoroughly enjoyed that job in New York. I had a good staff, I guess about 12 officers and a number of civilian inspectors. We were responsible for all the fire control equipment being built in the whole New York area. So it meant mostly Ford, Arma, Sperry, Control Instrument Company, AT&T and a lot of small outfits making various things.*

Q: Could you discuss each place and the kinds of things you did there? For example, Ford.

Admiral Walker: Ford was the manufacturer of all main battery and antiaircraft battery fire control computers. They also manufactured all of the gun control instruments, the elevation indicator-regulators, and the train indicator-regulators. Sperry was making the Mark 14 20-millimeter sight. Arma was making 100% submarine torpedo data computer systems. Westinghouse Elevator, they were making some component parts of some kind, but they weren't making any complete instruments. There was a small company, Watson Elevator, that was making the surface or the bridge ship bearing indicator for use with the torpedo data computer. When it first came out, there was no transmitter to transmit bearings from the bridge to the computer. In peacetime, we had never done any training whatsoever in nighttime operations in submarines. And, of course, that was a whole new ball game after the war started, because they needed something to get those bearings from the bridge to the data computer. And this Watson Elevator Company was building those torpedo target bearing indicators, as they were called. AT&T was building an experimental all-electronic main battery computer.

---

*AT&T--American Telephone and Telegraph Company.

During this period when I was naval inspector of ordnance at Ford, I was also inspector for IBM. They were building the Mark I antiaircraft computer, which had been designed by Ford, and they were using Ford drawings. Sometimes IBM thought they knew more about building it than Ford did, which caused some dissension at times. I made several trips to the IBM factory in Binghamton, New York, where the computer was being built. I was much impressed by their machine shop. The floors were all polished hardwood with a pan under each machine to catch any metal shavings or oil drip.

During one of my trips there, IBM was holding a dinner for the so-called sales engineers. That was undoubtedly the darnedest meal I ever attended. All the people at the dinner had songbooks filled with songs praising Ma and Pa Watson. I think they sang most of the songs in the book. The next morning, I had breakfast with Mr. Watson.* It was very interesting. He was telling about all his problems getting started in New York.

My naval inspector at IBM was a chief warrant officer. As you probably know, Mr. Watson was an ardent prohibitionist, and nobody at IBM ever admitted taking a drink. One day I got a call from the general manager at Binghamton telling me that my inspector had been seen going into a bar, and people at IBM didn't do that. I had to explain to him that my inspector did

---

*Thomas J. Watson, founder and chairman of International Business Machines (IBM).

not work for IBM. He worked for the U.S. Government, and he was free to go into a bar any time he was not on duty.

As an item of interest, I don't think IBM knew anything about computers until they built the Mark I antiaircraft computer. Of course, that was an analog computer, rather than a digital computer which they later developed. But I think their experience with the Mark I antiaircraft computer interested them in computer technology.

I remember going to Boston on an inspection trip, and at MIT I was shown and given a demonstration of a digital computer which was being developed at that time. It took a large room, at least 20 feet by 20 feet, filled with wooden racks on which were mounted vacuum tubes to operate the computer.

I was also inspector for AT&T. They were developing an electronic main battery fire control director. I remember going to their big building on West Fourth Street in New York City to observe the progress they were making. The whole project died at the end of the war.

Q: What does an ordnance inspector do? What was your job?

Admiral Walker: My job was to see to it that my inspectors inspected all the equipment and met the specifications. Or if there was a dispute between the inspectors and the people down in the shop that were building it, then I had to go up to the boss and talk turkey to him, tell him what he had to do. And that was it.

Q: Did they inspect each individual piece of gear or spot check?

Admiral Walker: They inspected each individual piece. They watched the computers being assembled and then, of course, they supervised all the checking and tests of it after the computer was assembled. I also had five or six WAVES as inspectors, the first time I had any contact with WAVES in the Navy.

Q: How well did they do in their jobs?

Admiral Walker: They did very well. And then for my administrative officer, I had W.T. Sampson Smith, grandson of Admiral Sampson, as my administrative officer. His father was R.C. Smith. He was also related to Rear Admiral W.T. Cluverius.

Q: Were the inspectors people with an ordnance background?

Admiral Walker: No. They were people with engineering backgrounds, not necessarily ordnance. Most of them were reserves.

Q: By and large, how capable were they?

Admiral Walker: They were very good. And then we also had a cost inspector, because all this stuff was built on cost-plus. Then I used to have to sign the checks for work progress. I remember the first time they brought a check to me for $2 million to sign, and I thought, "Oh, my God." Then I said to myself, "Well, what the hell?" And after that, I could sign them without even thinking about them. If it had been $500, I'd have been scared to death because then they might have got it out of me if I had done something wrong. But if it was $2 million, so what? They couldn't get blood out of a turnip. I didn't worry about $2 million.

Q: Were you, as part of your job, concerned about seeing that they kept to a certain schedule and produced things on time?

Admiral Walker: That is correct. Yes, we did.

Q: And generally did they adhere to the schedules?

Admiral Walker: They did very well, yes.

Q: Who established these schedules?

Admiral Walker: The Bureau of Ordnance gave us a schedule of when they wanted things and where they were to be shipped, and then we followed that.

Q: So I presume they were keeping track of the submarine construction and the surface ship construction and all that.

Admiral Walker: Oh, yes.

Q: Well, anything else about that job that springs to mind?

Admiral Walker: One of the jobs of the inspector, in peacetime and before there were very many ships being built, was to sign all the drawings that the contractor made to help build all these machines. Well, jeepers, every morning you'd be called to sign a stack of blueprints this high, and I said to myself, "This is a bunch of foolishness." So I had one of these pantographs made up, and after that, my top WAVE signed all the drawings for me. That was her main job, signing drawings for me. By the way, she was quite a gal. She caught multiple sclerosis while I was there, and I made arrangements for her to see the best doctor in that business in New York, and he told her that she had it, no doubt about it, and he gave her about ten years to live. She was out to our house a lot, and her boyfriend used to come and see her once in a while. Anyway, she got married, she raised three children, and she's still going. She's quite a gal.

Q: That's one doctor's prognosis you're glad turned out wrong.

Admiral Walker: Right.

Q: How demanding a job was that in terms of hours?

Admiral Walker: Not bad. You'd get in the office around 8:00, 8:30, and leave around 5:00, 5:30 in the afternoon. We weren't working nights usually, or when we were, there was no need for me to be there. And then, about every two or three months, I'd go to Washington for a conference with the people in the fire control section in the Bureau of Ordnance, on how things were going, any problems that they had I could help on, or anything they wanted done as far as their procurement business was concerned. And that was it.

Q: It sounds like it was just a case of managing a going concern at that point.

Admiral Walker: That's right. That's right. I'd taken over from a man in '22, Harold Baker.* He was a naval inspector of ordnance before me up there. But that was an excellent job, and I thoroughly enjoyed it. I had sold my car when I left Pearl Harbor, and I didn't have another automobile until the fall of

---

*Captain Harold D. Baker, USN.

1947. I was over five years without an automobile, and so any place I had to go in an automobile, one of my friends had to take me. But I was fortunate. I lived right close to Ray Crook, who was the chief liaison officer of the company, between Ford Instrument Company and the bureau, and so he saw to it that I got a ride whenever I needed it, which was very convenient. I had a government car, a Ford station wagon, to visit the companies I was responsible for.

Q: Did you have any encounters with Admiral Hussey during your visits to Washington?*

Admiral Walker: Once in a while I'd go in and see him, say hello to him, yes.

Q: Any impressions of him that you might have?

Admiral Walker: He was a great guy. He was an excellent man. He did an awful good job, I thought, as chief of the bureau. He was very pleasant, he was easy to deal with, he was very fair and very reasonable, a real good man.

Q: And very competent technically, I take it.

---

*Rear Admiral George F. Hussey, Jr., USN, Chief of the Bureau of Ordnance.

Walker #2 - 243

Admiral Walker: That is correct. Yes, very competent.

Q: Do you have any specific impressions of Sperry? We haven't talked in too much detail about them.

Admiral Walker: I had an assistant inspector out there, and I used to go out there about once every two or three weeks. I always got good cooperation from Sperry. I'll never forget, one year they were being renegotiated for their contracts, and that year Sperry had sold something like $400 million to the government, small money compared to nowadays. They made a profit of $70 million, so I was asked to come to Washington and appear before the renegotiation board. The board had finally decided that they would allow Sperry a profit of either $25 or 30 million, and it all depended on what I had to say. And they asked me what kind of cooperation I was getting from Sperry Corporation, and I said I had been getting excellent cooperation from them, no problems whatsoever; they'd been doing a good job. So they allowed them to make $30 million profit instead of $25 million profit, that's it.

Q: Five million on your say-so.

Admiral Walker: Yes. I don't think anybody at Sperry ever knew that.

Walker #2 - 244

Q: Probably just as well, or they might have tried to influence you.

Admiral Walker: Yes.

Q: What sorts of things did you do for recreation during that period? Did you get a chance to get away at all?

Admiral Walker: No. I didn't get any recreation except what little you might get over for a weekend and doing chores around the house; that was the only recreation I ever got, except that I played golf several times with Mr. Anderson, president of Watson Elevator Company.

Q: How much did you keep up with the progress of the war on the various fronts?

Admiral Walker: Just reading the papers, that's all.

Q: Did you have a chance to get any special briefings, say, on how the submarines were doing?

Admiral Walker: No.
I was detached in October of '45. The war was then already over. I was ordered to the West Coast to take command of the

Effingham (APA-165). She was in the yard at Mare Island and was being overhauled after her last voyage and so forth. She had had a civilian reserve merchant marine officer as skipper. Boy, the ship was filthy. I had a terrible time getting it cleaned up. I was being sent out to the Orient to pick up the people who had had enough points and were ready to come home, also to take out a whole bunch of boots to replace the people out there that had the number of points to come home. And just before I left, I got called up to the Western Sea Frontier operations office. The operations officer happened to be my good old friend Harry Sanders, who had been with me in the R-8, and he said two things.* First, my orders said for me to take the Great Circle course to Japan. Well, this was January. I said, "Harry, this is a bunch of foolishness. I don't want to go up around Alaska here in the middle of winter. How about if I just take the 30th parallel straight out to Japan?"

He said, "Okay, do what you're doing." Then he said, "I've got a job for you."

And I said, "What's that?"

"Well," he said, "you know this Japanese submarine skipper who sank the Indianapolis has been here, and we've been interrogating him and so forth. You've been designated to take him back to Japan."

"Well, no," I said, "what are the conditions involved?"

---
*Captain Harry Sanders, USN.

He said, "All we say is that you've got to get him there without any problem."

So they delivered him to the ship just before I sailed, and I put him in a padded cell, just so he couldn't kill himself. I was afraid he might commit suicide. So I put him in a padded cell, and he made the whole trip to Japan in that. We used to take him out twice a day and handcuff him to one of his guards, and we'd let him walk the deck for exercise. And I never talked with him. I couldn't speak any Japanese, and he couldn't speak any English, so I never did get to talk. But I'd just nod and say hello to him as he was walking around the deck. He was quite a character.*

Q: No interpreters along, I take it.

Admiral Walker: No. No.

Q: Did you just feed him the regular American rations?

Admiral Walker: Just fed him regular American rations, that is correct.

---

*The officer who sank the Indianapolis (CA-35) on 29 July 1945 was Lieutenant Commander Mochitsura Hashimoto, Imperial Japanese Navy, commanding officer of the submarine I-58. Hashimoto was taken to Washington to testify in the court-martial of Captain Charles B. McVay III, USN, commanding officer of the Indianapolis. Hashimoto was later the author of a book, Sunk: The Story of the Japanese Submarine Fleet, 1941-1945 (New York: Henry Holt, 1954).

Walker #2 - 247

Q: Did he seem generally cooperative?

Admiral Walker: Yes, he did. I think I could have just let him loose, as I thought afterwards, but I just didn't want to take any chances with it. It was a nice, comfortable padded cell that we had.

Q: He was virtually a prisoner, then, it sounds like.

Admiral Walker: Yes, yes. And then I went into an anchorage just off Yokosuka and sent him ashore to somebody, I forget now, who took charge of him, and I never saw or heard of him again.

Q: How long a trip was it?

Admiral Walker: I guess ten or 12 days, something like that. I don't remember exactly. I remember we passed one floating mine on the way out, and we shot that and exploded it. Otherwise, that was the only incident. Then we dropped off all the boots in Yokosuka, Japan. They'd done a good job. I got the ship just shining clean by the time I got to Japan.

Q: You had some sort of involuntary labor there.

Admiral Walker: That's right, but they really did a good job.

Walker #2 - 248

Then we went from Yokosuka up to Inchon. Well, that's quite a place. You have 16-foot tides, so we were anchored out in the river and during high tide, we'd take a boat in to the dock, but at low tide, if we left the boat in there, it was high and dry. You'd have to wait for the tide to come in again before you could go out. So while I was at Inchon, I made a trip up to Seoul. The Army supplied me with a staff car, and one of my officers went up with me. About halfway up to Seoul from Inchon, there was a great big mound of brass receptacles of all kinds, dishes, that the Japs had taken out of China and brought there to melt down for cartridge cases for ammunition. So I went through that thing, and I got a couple of orange crates full of various sizes, types, and so forth, of these brass bowls. As a matter of fact, we've got a couple of them down in the living room that we've got plants in. I've still got some more in bowls in the cellar, and I've given some of them to my children. It was really something. The pile must have been 15, 20 feet high and probably 30, 40 feet wide at the base. It's the biggest pile of stuff you ever saw. Then I spent the rest of that day looking around Seoul and then came back to Inchon. I didn't stay overnight. And then from Inchon, we went over to the Taku Bar just off Tientsin. Well, the water is so shallow there, you have to anchor out about 20, 25 miles from the beach. So I went ashore there in my gig. It was winter and so cold the engine's cooling system got clogged up with ice, and I thought, "Oh, my God, I'm out here in the middle of nowhere and no one knows exactly where I am." Of course, the ship had known where I'd gone. But finally we cleared the ice out of the circulating system and went on to Tientsin. I think I had one or two of my officers with me. Anyway, I remember we went to lunch somewhere in Tientsin and that was the most expensive lunch I ever had. It was $15,000.

Q: Oh?

Admiral Walker: I think it actually amounted to about $2.00.

Q: You mean these were 15,000 Chinese dollars.

Admiral Walker: That's right, 15,000 Chinese dollars. And then we picked up a load of Marines there at Tientsin, and we brought them back to San Francisco. I unloaded there. We went to San Diego, and from there we got orders to be decommissioned and to go to Norfolk. So we left San Diego for Norfolk, and we were only a day or two out of San Diego when one of my sailors fell down a hatch and landed on his head. So I got hold of a doctor. The doctor said, "I think I can pull him through all right. I don't think we need to go back to the hospital or get a plane to come out." So I took his word for it, and sure enough, he did, he pulled through, and they put him in a hospital in Panama when we got there, and I understand he completely recovered, for which

I was very pleased.

From Panama, we went to Norfolk, and I decommissioned the ship there.* I went home for about 15 days' leave and was ordered to command the tanker Elokomin. Well, she was in New York. A classmate of mine, Harry Henderson, had command of her, and I took command of the Elokomin, and we went to Argentia and dropped off a load of oil.** And then from there, we went to Baytown, Texas, to pick up another load of oil, and on the way back coming through the Florida Straits, one of my boilers burned out. So they sent me to the Boston Navy Yard, and I was in there in the summer of '46, sitting around, fat, dumb, and happy, and enjoying myself while waiting for them to repair the boiler. We'd taken a cottage down on the south shore right near where Bob Watson lived. We were having a pleasant summer when, all of a sudden one day, I get a telephone call from Bureau of Personnel—to leave within two or three days to take command of the Canisteo. She was scheduled for Operation Highjump in the Antarctic, and it seems that the commanding officer of the Canisteo was a classmate of mine, Bill Kirten. They had just discovered that his wife probably had cancer, and so he had asked to be relieved.*** Well, so what could I do? I didn't have much choice in the matter. When I got down there and found the

---

*The USS Effingham was decommissioned at Norfolk 17 May 1946.
**Captain Harry H. Henderson, USN.
***Captain William Kirten, Jr., USN.

situation, I was very unhappy. The operation was divided into three groups; the central group was to go into Little America, and the eastern group was over scouting the north coast of Antarctica and the southern group was scouting the south coast. Each group had a seaplane tender, a destroyer and an oil tanker. The commander of the group was Admiral Cruzen.* The so-called honorary commander was Admiral Byrd.** And he came down in the middle of the operation on a carrier and then went back on the carrier. He actually didn't do anything. But the unfortunate part was, I was senior to my group commander, who was George Dufek, of my class, but he was an experienced Antarctic sailor, and, of course, I knew nothing about the Antarctic.*** So they didn't change the command setup, but it was an unfortunate situation. Of course, this was the time when one of the seaplanes crashed into the Antarctic continent, and they finally saved about three or four of the crew and a couple of them died. (The captain of the Pine Island, Captain Howard Caldwell in '26, was aboard the crashed seaplane. He was saved.)**** On my way down there, I saw my first iceberg, and I fueled all the ships

---

　　*Rear Admiral Richard H. Cruzen, USN, Commander Operation Highjump, who was the officer in tactical command. For a book devoted to the subject of the 1946-1947 expedition, see Lisle A. Rose, Assault on Eternity (Annapolis: Naval Institute Press, 1980.)
　　**Rear Admiral Richard E. Byrd, USN (Ret.), noted antarctic explorer.
　　***Captain George J. Dufek, USN, commander of the eastern task group for Operation Highjump.
　　****Captain Henry Howard Caldwell, USN.

before they took the channel into Antarctica. Then I went over around Peter the First Island, acting as radio relay in communications for the planes while they were flying over the Antarctic continent. That was the time that Dufek was making a transfer from the Pine Island, which was the aircraft tender, to a destroyer, HMS Gimber—a high-line transfer—and the high line broke, and dropped him in the drink. He just barely survived, because you can't stay in that water very long. That water's about 30 degrees and you can't last very long. But the destroyer quickly cut loose, made a turn, came around, dropped over a motor whaleboat, and picked him up in a very short time. They gave him a good, hot shower and the doctor of the destroyer gave him a couple of shots of booze, and everything was all right.

Q: What was the source of your unhappiness—this command arrangement?

Admiral Walker: Yes. While we were down in the Antarctic, no problem. But on the way back, my group stopped in Rio.* Well, he was the senior officer present, not me, but I was senior to him. And we went to several parties; at one party he made a speech and he was a little bit tipsy. And when we got back to Norfolk, as we were coming up the channel, a boat came alongside, and the officer said, "When you get to your anchorage, nobody's

---

*Rio de Janeiro, Brazil.

to go ashore until further notice." And so the next thing I know, I was called before the admiral. He wanted to know what went on down in Rio. Apparently, the ambassador had made an adverse report on our stay there.

Well, I said, "Admiral, I see no excuse for this operation in peacetime. They said they put me in this job because I was the only experienced tanker commander. But I see no excuse in peacetime for putting a junior officer over a senior officer."

While we were there in Brazil, the Brazilian Navy gave us a party at the Brazilian naval officers' club, and Dufek made a speech. He rambled a little bit and so forth, and so the admiral wanted to know if Dufek was drunk. Also, he lost his hat one night while he was there, and it was discovered the next day in a house of ill repute.

Q: So you made this explanation to the admiral?

Admiral Walker: Yes, and I said it put me on the spot. What could I do? I said, "No, I don't think he was drunk, but I think he had plenty to drink." I wouldn't say he was drunk, no. Well, it must have all blown over, because Dufek was made admiral and I wasn't.

Q: What sorts of operations did you do down there other than what you've mentioned, the refueling and the radio relay?

Admiral Walker: That's about the extent of it. We were down there 99 days from Panama to Rio. We'd move around from time to time and from place to place. They'd want to push in a little different area, but it was all in the general area of Peter the First Island. And I remember one night we were moving from one location to another, steaming along at 15 knots, and I was up on the bridge, and I found the radar wasn't working. So I slowed right down immediately to five knots because you don't know-- there's all kinds of icebergs down there. If you hit one of those icebergs at 15 knots, no good. And you had a lot of reserve officers, and they weren't too observant at times. And this thing must have been off for I don't know how long. Nobody told me. If I hadn't been just snooping around to see what was going on, I'd have never found out. You just run into those kind of things, especially right after the war.

Q: Ships were generally undermanned at that time.

Admiral Walker: That's right. That's right. In general, I had a bunch of nice kids, but they weren't too experienced.

Q: Which isn't their fault.

Admiral Walker: No, they can't help it. They can't help it at all.

Q: But it sounds like a sort of a boring existence. What did you do to pass the time?

Admiral Walker: Mostly read and go to the movies. I'd go to the movies about every afternoon. Nothing else to do. And I had one guy from some nature outfit, and he was down there counting whales. He knew some Portuguese, so he used to come up to my cabin in the afternoon, and we'd have Portuguese lessons to get ready for Rio. And then we sent out a little expedition to the ice shelf; we picked up a few penguins and let them run around the ship for a while. We also caught some birds in nets.

Q: Were there any special precautions necessary since you were operating in colder weather than the Navy usually does?

Admiral Walker: Oh, yes, mostly special clothing, which we didn't have any of at all. And down there, it was amazing. The temperature rarely changed from 30. You see, this was Antarctic summer. You could see great big icebergs, and every once in a while you'd come across one of these big flat sort of icebergs, maybe half a mile long in diameter, just broken loose from the sea shelf and floating.

On the way back, we went over by the Palmer Peninsula and then up past Cape Horn and down into the Weddell Sea on the other side of the Palmer Peninsula. It was getting into March and

Walker #2 - 256

beginning to get toward the Antarctic winter. I remember one night cruising down there. I had at least 100 icebergs on my radar scope at one time, and we were just going along, five or ten knots, slow speed, just weaving our way through these icebergs. It wasn't so bad in the daytime; you could see them. But even then, you have to give them good berth, because some of them extend out quite a bit underwater from the part that you see above water, so you have to be very careful to give them a very wide berth.

Q: Did you have any problems pumping oil in that cold weather?

Admiral Walker: No, no, because we had heaters.

Q: Where had you gotten your training in how to run a replenishment ship? This was the first time you had any duty of that sort.

Admiral Walker: I just picked it up from the chiefs and the officers.

Q: Just the way you learned to be a destroyer man.

Admiral Walker: That's right. On the way down, we had stopped at Aruba to pick up a full tank of oil on the way. When I got into Colon, Panama, I was drawing about 32 feet of water. They assigned me an anchorage berth of 25 feet.

Q: So what did you do?

Admiral Walker: I said, "Hey, come on! I'm drawing 32 feet of water! Find me another anchorage."

Q: One of your friends was along on that operation. Jim Ogden was the navigator in the Philippine Sea with Admiral Byrd on board.*

Admiral Walker: Was he? I didn't realize that. I never saw the Philippine Sea. When she came down, she brought some mail for us. I don't know when I got that, but finally somehow it was delivered to me, and that was the only mail we got the whole time we were down there, but she just came around, down, and moved some planes off to the Little America and got them back and went back home. So she wasn't there any length of time.

Q: There was a submarine there, the Sennett.

Admiral Walker: That's right.

---

*Commander James R. Ogden, USN, whose Naval Institute oral history provides some discussion on the Philippine Sea's role in Operation Highjump.

Q: Did you refuel her at all?

Admiral Walker: Yes, I refueled her near Castle Island before she started in the channel for Little America. She never made it. There was too much ice. She got all clogged up with ice, and they almost lost her. And some of the AKAs got pretty well bashed up going through the ice there. We had the <u>Northwind</u> there as the icebreaker with us.

Q: All in all, it sounds like a dreary experience.

Admiral Walker: Oh, it was. There wasn't much for me to do. At least I didn't have many reports or anything to worry about. They couldn't get them to me, and I couldn't send them to them.

Q: Were your orders then coming from Admiral Cruzen? Would he tell the ships where to go each day?

Admiral Walker: Not each day, but every once in a while he'd change your position. We got very few orders, almost none.

Q: One thing I wanted to ask you about from when you were in the <u>Effingham</u>, who controlled your movements in the Far East? Was that the Seventh Fleet Commander?

Admiral Walker: I assume so. I don't remember. It must have been. All I know, is that when we were in Yokosuka, I got orders to go to Inchon. When I was in Inchon, I got orders to go to Taku Bar and pick up Marines from Tientsin. I was full up when I brought the whole crowd back. I had about 1,500 Marines on board.

Q: Did you have the same experience in the oilers that you had had in the transport of having to get the ship in shape after you took command?

Admiral Walker: No, no. They were both in nice shape. Both had been commanded previously by classmates of mine, and they were both in good shape. There's a sequel to that. Shortly after I had left for the Antarctic, about the seventh or eighth of November, Miriam went to the Army-Navy game in Philadelphia, and there was Bill Kirten and his wife, and my wife was mad as hell. There I was gone for five months in the Antarctic, and there they were out at the Army-Navy game.

Q: Did it turn out she had cancer after all?

Admiral Walker: I think so, yes. I don't remember. I never heard afterwards.

Q: Is there anything else about that stop in Rio that you remember other than George Dufek and his speech?

Admiral Walker: No, except that we were very well taken care of. We gave a party for the Brazilian brass aboard the Pine Island, which were all there. I had a Brazilian naval lieutenant aboard as a sort of liaison officer for me all the time I was there. When I left, he gave me a beautiful book about Brazil. I've still got it somewhere. I don't know where it is now. But it was a beautiful book about Rio.

Q: Did your Portuguese lessons do you any good?

Admiral Walker: Yes, I got so I could get along a little bit. At least this lieutenant could speak English, so I didn't have to, but I found I could get the drift of what was going on when I was with civilians. I never was a linguist in any case. I don't remember anything more outstanding about the Rio visit. I remember the dinner at the officers' club ashore and the party given on the Pine Island. That's about it. And then we returned to the States, and I picked up a load of oil somewhere--I guess it was back in Aruba--and brought it up to Norfolk.

And I hadn't been there very long when I was ordered to Bahrain Island in the Persian Gulf to pick up a load of oil and bring it back. So off we went to Bahrain Island. That was my first trip through the Suez Canal and around up into the Persian Gulf. We were there in Bahrain Island a couple of days. That's the hottest place in the world; the sun just beats down. All you could do was lay out on deck under an awning in a pair of skivvies and hope to keep somewhat cool, because the ships in those days had no air-conditioning. And then came back through the Suez Canal. It's strange, you know, in the Suez Canal under clear conditions, you can actually see the curvature of the earth. It's amazing. And then we brought the oil back. I think I delivered that also to Norfolk.

Then I got orders to the Bureau of Ordnance in Washington, and I was assigned as the senior Navy member of the Army-Navy Explosives Safety Board. Well, I went over there and started to learn something by perusing all their records about the problems of explosive safety in all the magazines throughout the country. But it was quite a bit of traveling. We weren't able to find a decent place to live in Washington. Miriam was still home with the children and her mother, so I went in to see the Chief of the Bureau of Ordnance. I said, "This is terrible. I don't like it a bit." I had a colonel who was the Army representative, and he acted like he owned the Army-Navy Explosives Safety Board, I told the chief of the bureau, "He does anything he damn pleases, and he never talks to me at all. I just don't want to be part of this."

So he said, "It looks like there's going to be an opening at postgraduate school. I'll send you down as head of ordnance at the Naval Postgraduate School," which he did.

We had to live out in town for a couple of months until my quarters became available. And then we moved into the yard and were there for the rest of the time, and that was about November of '47, and I stayed at the PG school until June of 1951. For the first two and a half years, Admiral Spanagel was the Superintendent, and he's a wonderful guy.* He and I were very simpatico and I got along well with him. Let's see. I was a third senior officer at PG school, after the exec, and it was a very, very happy and enjoyable tour of duty until he left, and then we got Admiral Herrmann.** Herrmann and I didn't see eye to eye.

Q: What about Admiral Spanagel made you work so well together?

Admiral Walker: I don't know. He was ordnance PG, same as I was. Herrmann wasn't. He was just very sympathetic with any ordnance problems I had. I also used to play golf with him every Sunday. That didn't do any harm. I was a lot better golfer then than I am now. I never was very good, but I was a lot better then than I am now.

Q: What sorts of duties were you involved in as head of the

---

*Rear Admiral Herman A. Spanagel, USN.
**Rear Admiral Ernest E. Herrmann, USN.

ordnance department there?

Admiral Walker: The title of the job was ordnance curriculum officer, and my main job was working up the curriculum for these various courses. We had the general ordnance, and we had fire control, we had missiles. The explosives people went off to universities, so we didn't have to fool too much with them. They went to the University of Michigan. The new missiles were just coming in. We'd give them a year at the PG school and then send them on a grand tour. We'd send them to a year at a university for some of the more exotic and new things. So I'd have to go to the colleges and arrange the curriculum for them. I had a lot of problems there at first 'til I learned what to do. But I would see the head of the department of these people, and then go over with him what the schedule should be, what studies. Well, they were always having fits because I wasn't allowing any time for electives. Well, I said, "The government isn't interested in electives. There is a certain body of knowledge that they want these people to have, and in the hours available, these are the things that we want them to study, and that's all there is time for." Well, they'd bitch about it, but finally they'd come around. Then they'd begin to say what they had to have before they would give them a degree. We finally ended up, I said, "By the time they have to have what you say you want them to have and the time I say, there's no more time for any electives." So finally they'd give in, set the courses up, and the boys would go and get their degrees.

Q: Tell me how you went about integrating the guided missile business into your curriculum.

Admiral Walker: Well, I was trying to think where we sent them. I can't remember the detail of it. But as far as we were concerned in PG school, it was just the basic sciences that would be applicable probably to missiles. Then it was the same way at the universities. It was the basic sciences that would probably be applicable to missiles, but it wasn't missiles as such.

Q: As you pointed out, when you went through the course, you were studying theory so you could become engineers.

Admiral Walker: That is correct. That's right. And that's what this was. And the thing was to try in all my talking with the university people, with the missile people, what sort of background in science should these boys have to be able to take and operate one of these programs later on after they graduated. But missiles as such, we didn't fool around with very much.

Q: Are there any of the professors that you had working there that you particularly remember?

Admiral Walker: Yes. I remember Terwilliger was an electrical engineering professor.* He had been electrical engineering professor when I went through the PG school. And also another electrical engineer who was nominated as my special assistant and liaison with the civilian professors. He was an electrical engineer; his name was Professor Wheeler.** I had quite a lot to do with the chemistry professor, and I can't remember his name, and also with the metallurgy professor, Professor Kinsler.*** In math, the head of the department was Professor Coates, who was excellent.**** But there again, my students had to take all these math courses, but I had nothing to do with planning these math courses and all. He was a real good mathematician.

Dr. Frye was head of the physics department.***** Professor Cavanaugh was an engineering professor when I was a student and when I was on the faculty.****** He was a real character. I believe he was the only professor at the PG School who didn't have an advanced degree. The first time I saw his act in the classroom, I thought he was drunk, but he wasn't.

All our instructors were civilian professors. We had about 80%-85% doctorate professors at the PG school. I was the senior

---
*Charles Van Orden Terwilliger.
**Richard Carvel Hensen Wheeler.
***Larry E. Kinsler.
****Wendell Coates.
*****Austin R. Frye.
******Dennis Cavanaugh.

Walker #2 - 266

line officer as a curricular officer, so I was on a council or whatever. It consisted of the civilian heads of departments, the superintendent, and the exec, and myself; it was like a Senate, you know.

Q: Was there any interchange at that time between the PG school and the Academy itself?

Admiral Walker: No. You know those three houses over there by the present Supply Corps building? Those three big houses, right near gate eight.

Q: Near the hospital.

Admiral Walker: This side of the hospital. We lived in the middle one. After I'd been there a short time, I was the fourth senior naval officer in the Naval academy and PG school. I was senior to every naval officer in the Naval Academy except the Superintendent. Of course, my superintendent of the PG school and the exec were senior to me, but I was senior to every officer at the Naval Academy.

Q: Was Annapolis a pleasant place to live in those years?

Admiral Walker: Yes, it was, a very pleasant place to live. Our first three months there before we moved into quarters, we lived in the Peggy Stewart House. Boy, that had a boiler in the cellar big enough to run a destroyer. What an outfit that was. And the day we moved into it, Commodore Greenman owned it, and he'd had a dog, and he had left it in the care of their colored maid.* The day we went into it, we had hardly started looking around and I was covered almost up to my hips with fleas. So the first thing we had to do was go down to the drugstore and buy three or four of these bombs, set them off in the house, and we went off to dinner. We came back about 9:00 or 10:00 o'clock, we never had a flea again in that house. And we had heard that the dog was a red cocker spaniel. His father was Red Brucy, and my mother was My Own Brucy. Boy, he was a pedigree from here to nowhere.

Q: Did you get around to the various ordnance centers in the country to find out what their needs were so you could direct your curriculum toward that?

Admiral Walker: No, no. While I was there, I did get sent to the big town in New Mexico right near Sandia, what's the name of the town? I forget. Well, anyway, I got sent out there for a week or ten-day course in special weapons.

---

*Commodore William G. Greenman, USN (Ret.). As a captain, Greenman had been commanding officer of the heavy cruiser <u>Astoria</u> (CA-34) when that ship was sunk by the Japanese in the Battle of Savo Island on the night of 8-9 August 1942.

Walker #2 - 268

Q: Did you have to get any special clearances for that?

Admiral Walker: Oh, yes, I had to get a Q clearance for that.

Q: Did you get any of the German rocket scientists working in any of the Navy programs?

Admiral Walker: They were, but they weren't working in connection with us at the PG school, no. They were working with, I guess it was Goddard Center and so forth, but they weren't working with us directly at PG school.

Q: Wasn't this about the time that the PG school was working to move out to the West Coast?

Admiral Walker: That is correct. About the middle of my tour there, the meteorology department was moved to the West Coast, and also the final closing of the deal to turn the Del Monte Hotel into a PG school was completed. Admiral Spanagel did all the work on that. He was the guy that put it through. He badgered Congress and everybody to get that done. If it wasn't for Admiral Spanagel, we never would have got the Del Monte Hotel and grounds.

Q: Did you move out there during your tour?

Admiral Walker: I went out there a couple of times to see what the physical situation was and what the arrangements were for our ordnance group out there. They still wanted to have a couple of 5-inch guns and so forth out there like we had used at the Naval Academy for people in the general line course, because there was going to be a general line school out there. As the ordnance officer, I was responsible for that, so we got the locations for a couple of 5-inch guns and practice and all that sort of thing. I made two trips out there for that purpose.

Q: Any of the students from that period that have later become prominent?

Admiral Walker: I was trying to think. I don't think so. There was one. I can't think. They all did fairly well, as far as I know. I don't know any of them who didn't do well.

Q: Was ordnance still considered a very desirable PG subject at that point, as it had been when you went through?

Admiral Walker: I think so, yes. I don't think it had quite the prestige that it did in the middle Thirties. Engineering was getting a lot of prestige at that time, building new high temperature boilers and all that sort of thing. And the biggest one was the radar and all electronics.

Q: Did you work with BuOrd also on what sorts of things should be included in the curriculum?

Admiral Walker: Yes, I'd go over and talk with the people over there, anything special I wanted.

Q: Anything else about the PG school you remember?

Admiral Walker: Let's see. That was very good living.

Q: Why do you say that?

Admiral Walker: Well, I had a beautiful set of quarters right where I could walk to work. I was very simpatico with the superintendent. The Superintendent lived on one side of me, and the exec lived on the other, three houses. One of the other heads of departments was a classmate of mine, John Melgaard.* After a year, John Melgaard was relieved by Tim Schultz in my class.** Captain Oberholtzer, head of meteorology was '26, and he went on to the West Coast first.*** Jack Fradd in '26 was the head of the engineering department.**** Bill Hollister in '30 was head of the aviation department.***** While I was at the

---
*Captain John L. Melgaard, USN.
**Captain William C. Schultz, USN.
***Captain William E. Oberholtzer, Jr., USN.
****Captain John E. Fradd, USN.
*****Captain William W. Hollister, USN.

PG school, my son was in high school and he wasn't doing very well in high school, so we sent him to Severn, that famous prep school, halfway between Annapolis and Baltimore.

Admiral Walker: As soon as he reached 16, I told him he'd better, if he had any interest at all in the Navy, he'd better join the Naval Reserve, because that gave him another string to his bow, just in case he missed out on the Presidential appointment, because he was doing so poorly in school, I had a hunch that he would never make the presidentials. So he did. He went about one year to high school, then he finished up his high school education at Severn School. I'll never forget, when he went to take the examination. Several days later, the head of the academic board they took for Presidentials called me and said, "Your son passed the Presidentials. He stood 50 in the group of 75 allowed."

I said, "I don't believe it."

He entered the Naval Academy in the summer of 1950, so during all his plebe year at the Naval Academy, I was right there at the PG school. He'd come home every Sunday, and—strange as it may seem—Carol Ann came over to visit us each Sunday, as plebes weren't supposed to drag.*

Q: Carol Ann was his girlfriend?

---
*Carol Ann Turner.

Walker #2 - 272

Admiral Walker: His present wife. So he'd come home to see Papa and Mama on Sunday, and Carol Ann would come to see Papa and Mama on Sunday, so that worked out well. Of course, they weren't supposed to ride in automobiles; even then midshipmen couldn't ride in automobiles unless they were a second classman or a first classman by then. But a couple of times it was raining hard, so Mother put him in the back of the car and put him down on the floor and would drive him back to the Naval Academy and drop him off over by the midshipmen's dorm, near the midshipmen's store. I said, "I won't do it, but if you want to, they can't do anything to you."

Q: It sounds like the Severn School was good for him.

Admiral Walker: It was. Yes, it was very good for him. I think he enjoyed being there. We bought him a jalopy that he used to drive himself to school. He did fine there. He played a little football.

Q: How did you get along after Admiral Herrmann came in and you didn't see quite eye to eye?

Admiral Walker: Well, we got along all right day to day, but it just wasn't the same happy situation it had been with Admiral Spanagel. Also we got a new exec about that same time, Captain

Walsh.* Harvey Walsh, class of '22. Joe Wright, J.M.P. Wright, was the exec when I first went there.**

Q: So then where from there?

Admiral Walker: In June 1951, I was detached from the PG School and ordered to command Destroyer Squadron 14. So I proceeded to Boston and relieved a good friend and classmate, Captain Swinburne, now Admiral Swinburne, as commanding officer of Destroyer Squadron 14.*** There's a little story about Swinburne. He and I entered the Naval Academy the same day, and he and I had decided that we were going to room together and we were both going to take Spanish. But when they talked me out of Spanish and back to French, then I had to get a new roommate, and that's when I got this roommate fellow named John Orr from Tennessee, my plebe year. How your lives intertwine together.

Q: You were with him on Admiral Withers's staff, too.

Admiral Walker: I was with him on Admiral Withers's staff, Admiral English's staff. So that's the way it goes.

Q: How many ships did you have in your squadron?

---
*Captain Harvey T. Walsh, USN.
**Captain Joseph M.P. Wright, USN.
***Captain Edwin R. Swinburne, USN.

Admiral Walker: We had eight ships. They were 2,300-ton long hulls.* During the whole year I had that squadron, I never had more than five ships of the eight with me at any one time. My flagship was having a short overhaul. We got out of the Navy Yard shortly after I took command and went to Newport, and then after a while in Newport, we went to Guantanamo Bay for a shakedown of the ship after the overhaul. We came back from that, and we had a cold weather exercise up around Greenland with Admiral Holloway in command.** And on the way back, we stopped in at Halifax for a few days' R&R.*** There wasn't too much outstanding about that that I can remember.

Q: What was your flagship?

Admiral Walker: The USS W.C. Lawe, the last of the 2,300-tonners to be decommissioned.**** She was just decommissioned up in the Great Lakes about a year ago.

Q: She'd been a reserve training ship.

---

*The ships were of the Gearing (DD-710) class, 14 feet longer than the 376-foot, 6-inch "short-hull" Allen M. Sumner (DD-692) class. The ships in the squadron included those in Destroyer Division 141--William C. Lawe (DD-763), Power (DD-839), Glennon (DD-840), and Everett F. Larson (DDR-830)--and the ones in Destroyer Division 142--Warrington (DD-843), William M. Wood (DD-715), Goodrich (DDR-831), and Perry (DD-844).
    **Rear Admiral James L. Holloway, Jr., USN.
    ***R&R--rest and recreation.
    ****USS William C. Lawe (DD-763).

Walker #2 - 275

Admiral Walker: Yes, that's right. I have a picture of her.

Q: Did you deploy to the Mediterranean at all?

Admiral Walker: No, no. That's where I found out really that my weakness as far as destroyer tactics and so forth was bad. I wished I'd had more training younger. If, instead of that destroyer squadron, I'd have gotten a cruiser, I wouldn't have had any problem at all. But being in command of a big screen with lots of maneuvering for destroyers that has to be done, as I say, I could just barely keep ahead of it by reading the book. I was always about a paragraph behind.

Q: Did you have a good chief staff officer you could rely on?

Admiral Walker: I had a chief staff officer who was a wonderful guy, but he didn't know from nothing. And I had an operations officer; he wasn't too smart. He didn't know as much about destroyer tactics as I did. I didn't have any Naval Academy officers who had been trained in destroyers at all to help me. It was most unfortunate. I think that's one reason probably that I didn't get an outstanding fitness report, although I've never looked to see. I didn't bother.

It was during that time that I was ComDesRon 14 that I was head of a couple of investigations of accidents. One was the grounding of a destroyer coming from Boston to Newport, an old 1,200-tonner. I happened to mention in the report that two or three people on the ship, key enlisted men, had missed their ship. And I determined that their absence had nothing to do at all with the grounding. So then I get a letter of hate signed by the admiral—of course, written by his stupid lawyer—wanting to know why I didn't investigate why those few people were absent. So I just wrote him back that the precept asked the board to determine why the ship went aground, not why somebody was absent. I don't think they liked that. The admiral approved the board's findings concerning the cause of the grounding.

Q: What ship was that, do you remember?

Admiral Walker: I don't remember. And then when we were down in Guantanamo, one of the ships there, I think one of the 1,700-tonners, shot off the barrel of its number two gun forward with the number one gun and killed a man on the bridge, and I was the chief investigator for that, although I never got any hates on that. I don't know if they were happy with the investigation I made, but I never heard from that one.

While Commander Destroyer Squadron 14, I had the pleasure of escorting the SS *United States* on her maiden voyage into New

York. I had five destroyers with me.* My flagship was the lead destroyer. There was one destroyer on each bow and one destroyer on each beam. We met the United States about 25 or 30 miles south of Ambrose Lightship, turned simultaneously and then escorted her into New York. It was a very magnificent sight with all the New York City fireboats shooting up streams of water as she came in. After she was berthed, myself and all my officers were invited to a delightful reception that afternoon aboard the United States.

Q: What do you remember about being on board the liner?

Admiral Walker: I remember that she was very plush and very beautifully appointed inside, and that the food was excellent.

Q: What kind of speed was she making as she came in, do you recall?

Admiral Walker: As I recall, she was making around 25 knots when we picked her up.

---

*The destroyers which served as escorts were the William C. Lawe (DD-763), Goodrich (DDR-831), Warrington (DD-843), Perry (DD-844), and William M. Wood (DD-715). The arrival of the United States at New York for the first time occurred on 23 June 1952 and was covered in considerable detail by the following day's issue of The New York Times.

Walker #2 - 278

Q: They needed pretty fast ships to keep up with her.

Admiral Walker: Oh, yes. Of course, she could go a lot faster than that, but she was making about 25 when we picked her up. We were headed towards her, and then I made a U-turn. The other two ships did, and we went into the port.

Q: Did you go out specially for that, or were you just in the area on maneuvers?

Admiral Walker: No, we were requested specially to escort her into New York on her maiden voyage. She was coming up from Newport News where she had been built. She had had trials off there, but this was her maiden visit to New York City.

Q: Was this purely a ceremonial thing, or was there some concern about her safety?

Admiral Walker: Oh, no, purely ceremonial. No thought of safety in those days.

Q: Were there any of your individual ship skippers from that squadron that you remember in particular?

Admiral Walker: Yes, I remember very well the skipper of

the Lawe, Commander Tom Suddath.* He's now dead; he was in the class of '39. And one other skipper that I knew quite well was Art Esch, in the class of '40, Admiral Esch.** His final duty, I believe, was commander of the Washington Naval Shipyard.

Q: Did any of your other skippers besides Esch make flag rank?

Admiral Walker: No, I can't think of any. I can't recall any. I had a division commander, I can't remember his name either, but I only saw him once during the year I had command. He was with his ship mostly in overhaul in Philadelphia, as I recall. He was up with me just once in Newport. He loved to make rugs and had a big frame in his cabin, and he made rugs.

Q: Who was ComDesLant at that time?

Admiral Walker: Spike Fahrion was part of the time, and Charlie Wellborn the rest of the time.***

Q: Is there anything you remember about either of those during that period?

---

*Commander Thomas H. Suddath, USN.
**Commander Arthur G. Esch, USN.
***Rear Admiral Frank G. Fahrion, USN; Rear Admiral Charles Wellborn, Jr., USN.

Admiral Walker: Not particularly, except I had nothing to do much with them except, as I say, where I told you about the endorsement on the investigation I made into the destroyer going aground and I didn't blame the admiral. But I don't think it helped me any.

Q: I got the impression that Fahrion was a pretty strict guy.

Admiral Walker: Yes, it was Fahrion's lawyer that wrote it, not Wellborn's. If it had been Wellborn's, I'd have stormed in and yakked at him. Of course, having had Wellborn as a squadron commander during the war, I knew Wellborn very well.

Q: So you probably had a good relationship with him when he was the type commander.

Admiral Walker: That is right. I did, yes.

Q: Did the destroyer officers tend to socialize together when you were in home port up in Newport?

Admiral Walker: Not too much, no. No. I generally made it a point to be on the beach when a heavy storm was coming, and if I couldn't get out the next morning with the ship, it was too bad. Because in those days, we didn't have piers for destroyers. We had to anchor out at the buoys. If there was a heavy storm, the possibility I wouldn't get ashore that night, I'd leave in time to get ashore, and if I couldn't get out in the morning 'til late or maybe all day, that was too bad.

Another interesting trip, I had three destroyers with me, and I was ordered to Portland, which, of course, was my home town, for a convention of the American Legion. The morning that we were due to arrive, a heavy fog set in about 6:00 o'clock. And we just had to creep our way into the harbor. I released the other two destroyers to come in on their own, and using radar, we went in until we met the tug coming out to meet us. This was around 9:00 o'clock. By 10:30, it was clear as a bell. Then I went up and called on the city manager. The head of the American Legion wanted me to parade my destroyers up and down the beach at Old Orchard. I told him, "No smoke." If the Legionnaires wanted to see the ships, they were more than welcome to come down and see the ships, but I certainly wasn't going to parade them off the beach at Old Orchard for them. They invited us out there, my wife and I and several other officers and their wives, and we were invited to several functions and dinners that the American Legion had on at Old Orchard.

At the end of a year, I got my orders to go to shore duty. While I was in Newport, the commanding officer of the naval base there asked me to be his chief of staff. He was one of the Olsen boys, Admiral Olsen. (By the way, he was a younger brother to another Olsen who was CO of the R-9, whom I knew when I was out in Pearl.*) All you were getting then was a year's tour as a destroyer squadron commander, so I said, yes, I'd be very happy to be his chief of staff, because I liked it around Newport.

Well, he sent a dispatch requesting orders for me, and they came back, "No smoke. Walker's being sent to command the naval mine depot at Yorktown." So that's where I went, and that was my last three years, and probably three of the happiest years I ever had in the Navy. That was just wonderful living. I had a wonderful set of quarters, I had a good steward, I had about 1,500 civilian employees, I had 500 Marines—more Marines than any other station on the Atlantic seaboard except Quantico and Camp Lejeune. I had about 500 sailors; I had about 100 officers.

Q: Why so many Marines?

Admiral Walker: Because they started building an annex to the mine depot while I was there, to store new weapons. We had 12,000 acres also to be patrolled. I had five horses for the horse Marines for patrol. Also we had a dairy there, and we used to get all our milk from the dairy at a very reasonable price until the local dairy people made us shut the dairy down. Oh, that was just wonderful duty.

---
*Rear Admiral Clarence E. Olsen, USN, Commander Naval Base Newport, 1951-1953. His brother, Charles E. Olsen, commanded the USS R-9 as a lieutenant in the late 1920s.

Q: You say you weren't too well suited for that DesRon job. Why weren't you given a chance at a submarine squadron?

Admiral Walker: I had no wartime experience in submarines. I knew I didn't have a chance. Anybody that was going to get a submarine squadron then would be somebody that had had war experience in submarines. While I had been attached to the submarine force for the first eight, nine months of the war, I had no actual duty in a submarine, and I knew that it was useless to even think about submarines.

Q: So that's maybe where you did get hurt by not going to that command rather than the staff at the beginning of the war.

Admiral Walker: As I say, if I had been fortunate enough to get a cruiser, I'd have had no problem at all.

Q: Had you expressed a desire for a cruiser?

Admiral Walker: I had asked for a cruiser, but I didn't get it. I got the destroyer squadron instead.

Q: They were both considered major commands.

Admiral Walker: That's right, they were. In some ways, a

destroyer command is more of a major command, because it's a multiple command; it's an eight-ship command. Just being the commanding officer of a ship is a relatively simple job. First of all, you've got an awful lot of good help in a big ship like that, which you didn't have in the destroyers right after the war.

Q: I've talked to officers who've commanded oilers as you did, and then went to cruisers, and they said the cruiser job was actually easier, because they had more talent to work with.

Admiral Walker: That's right. That's what I was hoping for, but my luck ran out.

Q: Had you expressed no desire to go to a war college at all in the years up to then?

Admiral Walker: No. As I say, during my formative years, when I might have liked to go, the only people who went there were those nobody else wanted.

Q: Afterward, though, that became a useful ticket to get promoted.

Admiral Walker: That's right. But it wasn't so some years

earlier. Just before I retired, when I was in Newport in command of the destroyer squadron, there were several people, friends of mine, that were going through the senior war college course. But I never asked for the war college; I never took any war college correspondence courses. That's the way it worked out.

Q: Could you go into more of the specifics on what you did down at Yorktown?

Admiral Walker: Yes. Well, it was a busy time, because we were the major storage depot for heavy explosives on the Atlantic coast. We stored all the heavy explosives. We had three TNT pouring plants. We loaded mines, torpedoes, bombs, and all that sort of thing. I forget how many magazines we had, but we had almost 100 magazines, I think, strewn around 12,000 acres.

Q: Was there a great emphasis on safety?

Admiral Walker: Yes, very much, especially in the TNT plants--I say TNT, but by that time it was modified to a more highly explosive substance than TNT. I forget the name of it that we were pouring, but most of the time we had only about two pouring plants in operation. They had one explosion there during the war and quite a few people were killed. My quarters were built like a fort almost. It had great big thick walls and thick floors.

When I got there, the houses on officers' row, which was a group of houses—my house was at the end and had big white columns out front. The other big ones down the line were for all the heads of departments. But they were all heated by coal with stokers, and a man used to come around every morning and check them out, take out the ashes, and fill up the stokers and so forth. I said, "This is a hell of a way to heat a house." One pipe steam with steam heating, which isn't so hot anyway. So I talked the bureau into the money to change the heating system to circulating hot water. Well, in my quarters, it really amounted to something. They had a terrible time drilling through the thick concrete floors, because they only had one pipe furnishing the radiator for steam systems, so they had to run up two pipes to have a circulating hot water system. And then I had the house zoned so that there were three zones to it, the downstairs, the upstairs, and then there was the stewards' quarters so each one could control its own heat. Everybody along that whole row was very happy to get that circulating hot water rather than the steam heat.

We had a nice little club there, sort of rustic. We had a little trouble keeping it solvent, especially in being able to support a manager to run it. But we were able to do it. We used to have a lot of social functions there. We had a swimming pool. When I got there, we had a five-hole golf course. There was a Seabee outfit in the supply depot just up the line, Cheatham

Annex, so I talked to the commanding officer of the Seabees to come down and exercise his troops and teach them how to use their equipment by building me four more holes so I'd have a nine-hole golf course.

Q: Why was your house so sturdily built?

Admiral Walker: I don't know, except they thought the Navy explosives might blow it up. It was really heavily built.

Q: You had a steward that sometimes people thought was you, didn't you?

Admiral Walker: Yes. His name was Walker. Of course, after a while, everybody knew who the steward was, but it nonplussed people a little bit at first.

Q: When Walker answered the phone, "Walker's house."

Admiral Walker: "Commanding officer's quarters. Walker speaking." He was the pride of the local colored gal population outside the gate, because he had four gold stripes. He was a chief steward. I had a pretty good thing. I was lucky. When I went to Yorktown, I made arrangements to get my steward transferred from the destroyer squadron flagship to Yorktown. My doctor transferred from the flagship to Yorktown, and my squadron chaplain transferred there. So I had somebody to look after my soul, I had somebody to look after my health, and I had somebody to look after my stomach. I was well taken care of.

Q: So Walker had been with you in the destroyer squadron also?

Admiral Walker: Yes. Then my second chaplain at Yorktown was Chaplain Trower, who just retired as Chief of Chaplains.*

Q: Your son was managing to make it through the Naval Academy without your help, then, after you left.

Admiral Walker: Yes. He came down to Yorktown several times. I was there in Yorktown from '52 to '55, so I was there two years, before he graduated in '54. And I remember one time he came down and it was duck-shooting season. And he was out shooting ducks right near one of my blinds, but also right near the national park, and one of the rangers picked him up for shooting on national park land. So I had to call up the head of the national park to get him out of hock.

Q: Did you have much dealing with the local community there as far as making the Navy a good neighbor in the area?

---

*Lieutenant Ross H. Trower, CHC, USN.

Admiral Walker: Well, we always participated very much in Yorktown Day. That's the date of the surrender of Cornwallis in Yorktown; they have it every year.* And we always had a contingent of Marines, and maybe one of our people would be the grand marshal. And, of course, we were under the Commander Naval Base Norfolk and also under the commandant at Norfolk. Well, shortly after I was there, President Eisenhower and his wife came down. He was going to make a talk at Williamsburg, and they landed at my pier in Yorktown. So I was down there with a Marine guard, and the admiral from the naval base was there and the commandant was there--all to greet the President. And then we had a cavalcade of cars to drive him to Williamsburg and bring him back. Miriam had a nice chat with Mrs. Eisenhower while she was there at the pier.

Q: Did you get to meet Eisenhower?

Admiral Walker: Oh, yes. Oh, sure. Yes, I was there to greet him.

Q: Any impressions of him that you have from that meeting?

Admiral Walker: Not really, except he seemed to be a nice guy.

---
*Lord Charles Cornwallis, the British commander, surrendered at Yorktown on 19 October 1781, essentially marking the end of the American Revolution.

Walker #2 - 290

A good grin, you know.

Q: So you had met two out of the three Presidents there. You missed only Truman in between.

Admiral Walker: That's right. That's right.

Q: Well, what was your day-to-day job as the commanding officer at Yorktown? What sorts of things did you do personally?

Admiral Walker: Personally, I went through correspondence every day. I had very little of it that I wrote. Most of the heads of the departments handled all the technical stuff, and writing their own letters and signing by direction. And then every morning I'd get a pack of letters that had been written the day before, and I'd go through them to see if there was anything that was not in accordance with policy. Once a week I had a meeting of all the heads of departments and gave them any special information I had that I thought might be of interest to them, and listened to any gripes that they had or any problems that they had. And then there were inspections. I spent a lot of time going all over the place. I'd go out and inspect the magazines, and I had special shoes to wear at the TNT plants. One interesting thing, on the naval mine depot, they had an old house that was the Lee house, and it belonged to the Lee family at one time. Nobody in the past had taken much interest in it and it was beginning to go to rack and ruin. But I understand since then some of the Lee descendents or some of the other groups in Virginia have really rehabilitated the place quite a bit. I haven't seen it since, of course. It was just out in the woods where the magazines were.

I had one incident while I was there. I used to have to go down and inspect the Marines. We had Marines on patrol in the magazine area. Some of them didn't care too much for that at night. It was sort of scary, completely dark out there, you know, in the woods. One morning one Marine came out to relieve another one, and just fooling around, he picked his pistol up, put it in the guy's chest, and said, "Stick 'em up." And he shot it. He didn't mean to, it was accidental. He accidentally shot him. Fortunately the Marine didn't die. But it seemed like things like that were coming up all the time.

Q: Did you employ your civilian work force mostly from the local area?

Admiral Walker: Local area. Also at that time we had a small hospital there with a staff of about four doctors and two nurses, and we had a couple of ambulances. We used to have to send them out quite often to pick up casualties of automobile accidents in the area and take them to the local hospitals and so forth.

Walker #2 - 292

Q: Was there any apprehension about making sure you had reliable people to work around the ammunition? Did you have any screening process?

Admiral Walker: Not particularly, no. I can't remember now. I wouldn't have handled it anyway. The personnel guy would handle it, and what he did, I don't know.

Q: I wonder if there would be any difficulty getting people who were willing to work in that kind of an operation? That's not for everybody.

Admiral Walker: No, but, of course, there's all kinds of shops and jobs--a carpenter shop, a metal-working shop and every kind of shop you could think of. We had mostly sailors, about 500 in the torpedo shop and mine shop. We had a force of about 1,500 civilian employees. Also, I had about 250 housing units I was responsible for, regular Navy housing and Wherry housing, and God knows what all. I had a housing officer that looked after the details of that; I didn't.

Q: The way you portray it, everybody else was doing the work and you were just in charge.

Admiral Walker: That is correct.

Q: It sounds like a good way to do it.

Admiral Walker: That's the way I've always worked.

Q: Who was your boss? Did you report to Com Five?

Admiral Walker: No, my immediate boss was Commander Naval Operating Station Norfolk. My exec was an officer by the name of Bunny Shupper, class of '37.* He retired as an admiral. I haven't seen Bunny since I left Yorktown. My last year, my exec was Commander Carl Cunningham.

Q: Anything else from that tour that we should discuss?

Admiral Walker: I was trying to think. Nothing I can think of except I had a very nice change of command ceremony when I was relieved. That was it. That's my career.

Q: Any overall thoughts on this career that you want to discuss at this point?

Admiral Walker: I thoroughly enjoyed my 30 years in the Navy, 34 years, including the Naval Academy. Some people don't understand it, but you're a part of the Navy when you become a midshipman,

---

*Commander Burton H. Shupper, USN.

because you're sworn in as a midshipman in the United States Navy, which is a recognized naval rank. Now when you go to West Point, you're sworn in as a cadet, U.S. Military Academy. You're not sworn into the Army at all until you graduate. That's the difference there. It's the same way at the Air Force Academy. You're sworn in as a cadet in the United States Air Force Academy; you're not in the U.S. Air Force.

Q: I didn't realize that.

Admiral Walker: Yes, that's the biggest difference. You're not sworn in as a midshipman in the United States Naval Academy; you're a midshipman in the United States Navy. At least that was the situation when I entered the Naval Academy.

Q: Had you done any explorations of the job market before your retirement?

Admiral Walker: Yes, I did a little, but I wasn't very successful. I liked the Tidewater area, and I would have liked very much to stay in that area. But there wasn't anything available I could find. They were building a new refinery down there in that area, but any job I could get wasn't anything I was really interested in. My brother-in-law, who was the secretary of VEPCO, had a very good relationship with their financial printer here in New York, Pandic Press.* And he arranged for me to have an interview with them, and it was arranged for me to have a management position with Pandic Press. Well, I came here to New York and started studying how the operation worked, and they wanted me really to become a salesman. I said, "No smoke." Then also, I discovered that as a manager in the printing business, you'd be working about half the night, because the banks and lawyers work all day, working up the prospectus that they send out when they're going to float a new issue. And they'd finish that up at 5:00 or 6:00 o'clock at night and turn it over to the printer, and they wanted it the next morning. So after fooling around with that for a little over a year, I said, "This is not for me." And we mutually agreed to break the relationship. And then for about six or eight months, I had nothing to do but look around.

Finally, I contacted an employment agency downtown in New York, and they were just about to start up an executive search firm. So I went with them, and it was known as Executive Manpower Corporation. Well, that was the late fall of '56, and I stayed with them until I reached 62 in October of '66, for ten years. And we grew to be a pretty good-sized executive recruiting firm. About the middle of the time I was there, Manpower, Inc., got up on their ear because we were using the word "Manpower." So about the middle of the time I worked for

---

*VEPCO—Virginia Electric Power Company.

them, they changed the name of the company from Executive Manpower Corporation to Executive Manning Corporation. But I would never advise anybody to go into executive recruiting unless you enjoy sitting on a telephone all day long. I couldn't reach 62 fast enough. I figured I might not live to be 65, to draw Social Security, but I could commence drawing Social Security at 62, and I was going to take it then along with my retired pay, I'd make out somehow. And I did. I retired. I reached 62 in October of '66, and I retired on October 30 of 1966. I haven't worked since.

Q: Well, what have you done? Surely something day-in and day-out.

Admiral Walker: Fortunately, shortly after I retired, about a year or so, I joined a group in Ridgewood known as Hobbyists Unlimited. It was started by a group of 16 men at the Presbyterian church here in Ridgewood. It started just about the time I retired. But I didn't know about it until about two years later, when a very good friend of mine, Captain M. Peirce Kingsley, who was a member of the church, told me about it after he retired--he didn't retire until he reached 65. He was the class of '23, but he was about five years older. Anyway, he didn't retire until just after this group was formed. So I joined them. We've grown from 16 members to 350 with a waiting list of 75, all retired men from all walks of life. We have a meeting once a month, and we have all these various groups. We have a bridge group, we have bowling group, we have a golf group, philately group, investment group, you name it, we've got it. Then in addition to that, we have trips and tours, some sort of trip or tour going on all the time--such as going to lunch and theater, or on a four or five day cruise in the Caribbean. We've got a cruise coming up in the Chesapeake here very shortly. Next Monday we're supposed to have a cruise on the Hudson River. If you want to, you can be busy all the time. I just don't have time. I now only play golf twice a week with the hobbyists on Tuesdays and Friday, we're on a regular schedule from April through the end of October every year. So I'm so busy, I just don't know what to do with myself. I can't find time to keep up with my reading, and I like to read The Wall Street Journal every day if I can. I enjoy dabbling a little bit in the market. I don't invest very much in any one thing at any one time. I have a lot of fun playing it. So far, I'm ahead of the game.

Q: I'm sure, too, that you've taken great pride in your son's achievements.

Admiral Walker: Oh, yes, I have. And we visited him at his duty stations. We visited him when he was in Panama, we visited him when he was in Rota, Spain. We used to see quite a lot of him when he was in Newport. We used to visit him in Norfolk, and we visited him in Key West when he was submarine squadron supply officer and supply officer of the Howard W. Gilmore. We went to see him in the New Jersey. We visited him in Norfolk, and then, of course, the children came along and we got interested in them.

Our daughter graduated from college in '59. She went to Hollins in Virginia, and she worked for about four years for Steuben Glass in their main office here in New York, and then she got married. She is now Mrs. Charles R. Reuning. Then she immediately went to Holland with her husband, and her first boy was born over there, and we went over there and visited with her in Holland several times during the two years she was there. After being in Holland for two years, they went to Belgium, to Brussels, in Brussels for a couple of years and we visited them there each year. And then they came back to California, and for three years in a row, we drove out to California and had Christmas with them in California. So not a dull moment.

Q: That's great. How much have you kept in touch with the Naval Academy Alumni activities?

Admiral Walker: Well, I used to go to the Alumni Day in the fall.

Q: Homecoming?

Walker #2 - 299

Admiral Walker: Homecoming in the fall. But I don't do it any more, but I make all the reunions. I've made all my reunions since the 25th.

Q: There's a special bond that develops among the classmates that lasts a lifetime.

Admiral Walker: There certainly is, yes. I have one classmate--he and I rowed together plebe summer--this guy that lived across the court from me whom I took out to Pearl Harbor on the morning of the attack; he's in Florida now.* His wife died a little while ago, and he's got Lou Gehrig's disease now, and he can hardly get around. He has to live in a wheelchair practically, but I see him every year when I go to Florida. So I'm busy all the time.

Q: I'm glad that I was able to fit into your schedule. This has been an enjoyable period for me to hear about your life, and I'm grateful to your son for recommending it.

---
*Rear Admiral Edward L. Beck, USN(Ret.)

Appendix

The following is a letter written in early 1943 from Commander E.R. Swinburne to his Naval Academy classmate, Commander Edward K. Walker. Walker had written from his ship, the USS Mayrant, to Lieutenant Commander Reilly Coll, of the staff of Commander Submarine Force Pacific Fleet. In the meantime, in late January 1943, Coll was killed in an airplane crash, so Swinburne answered instead. Particularly interesting is the paragraph on page two which discusses tests conducted to determine the suitability of a "down-the-throat" torpedo shot which had been suggested by Commander Walker.

SUBMARINE FORCE, PACIFIC FLEET

Care of Fleet Post Office,
San Francisco, California,
February 11, 1943

Dear Ed:

After holding your letter to Reilly for a couple of days, I decided to open it rather than send it on to Margaret. As it is, I can attempt to answer a good many of the questions you raised.

I left here on Christmas Day to go to the coast for a change of scenery and prepare people for the Admiral's inspection at Mare Island and San Diego. Early in January, the Admiral and Jiggs made a trip to Midway. In the meantime, Jiggs was ordered to Mare Island and Bill Myers was selected as his relief -- Bill having just returned from a month in San Diego (had had prostrate trouble which necessitated his relief in Gato). Then Buships wanted Jiggs and Bill at a conference with Kent Loomis, Beltz and others in Washington. Pete Ferrall was to meet them in San Francisco, look over the activities in Bay area with them and join the entourage. Sparky Woodruff (as Flag Lieut) was going with the Admiral but Reilly volunteered to be the aide for the trip in order to be able to see Margaret in Washington (Margaret left Louisville and went on, taking a place at 806 Hillgrove Ave, Church Falls, Virginia where she is now). Bob Smith was relieved by Vic Blue in Sperry, and became CSS 2, proceeding to Mare Island where all that squadron is overhauling (Duke was acting CSS 2 but has now gone to general service and Swede Momsen is CSS 2 with Joe Connolly as CSD 22 and K.C. Hurd, relieved in Seal, and acting CSD 21).

The party left here on January 20 and were in a PAA plane piloted by Chicken John's cousin -- he had been in New Zealand run and only been into San Francisco twice before. It was a lousy day to arrive -- ceiling about 3500-4000, heavy rains, 35-40 wind with puffs of 55-60. Connolly, Ferrall and I were waiting on Treasure Island. No radio after 0715 and PAA practically gave up then although we waited around until 1800. Evidently the plane crashed near Ukiah enroute Clear Lake about 0730. Fire destroyed all papers they were carrying. The plane wreckage covered a large area. Carmick escorted the bodies east; Gene Crane, Sue Myers and Cookie Grenfell also. Jiggs was buried in Annapolis alongside Jackie, while Bill Myers was buried in Arlington. Don't know about the others. "Alice" Black (Cincpac personnel) class of '26 was also on board. Sue Myers was quite unnerved, but Gene Crane was quite o.k.

Harry Maynard is acting 90 -- he was gunnery in Holland. Joe Grenfell is 70 and tactical, and Weary wants to order him to 70. Garrison went on a cruise in Tunny and Sparky is 15 and 20. While I was on leave, Joe was 12 (tactical), 20, 70 and 90, while Sparky was 05 and 15. When I returned I found I had an assistant.

- 1 -

SUBMARINE FORCE, PACIFIC FLEET

Brady is Exec. in the American Legion a transport somewhere.

Maynard read your letter. He and Patrick (Despac gunnery) are working out the final plans for rigging necessary screens and conducting your zero track problem with a 6 exploder in an exercise head. Am sending you a copy of Wahoo patrol report -- you will be particularly interested in the actual war test. Mush Morton did all you requested -- he is a big hero and has not bought a larger hat. Will send you any dope we get on trials here. Your points are well taken Ed, but can we be sure Jap DDs have same turning characteristics as Mayrant? I think some of the skippers would rather try it on rehearsals than plan to use it in actual practice unless in a last extremity when they are caught short.

Chester Bruton wants to be 05 and I am ready to go -- the last of the old crowd and I miss you all as much as you probably miss subs. The twenty first was a blow, Ed, and packing up Reilly's effects was not like going to a circus. Have no idea what I can get although Captain Brown told me the Admiral was going to recommend me for CSD 41. I still believe the more recent ex skippers rate it more. However, Knapp, Pace and Peacher have new divisions; Red Stevens is going east to a divcom job; Karl Hensel has 101; Bill Suits has 81; Owen Humphreys and Fred Warder are here waiting for someone to die while Chet Smith is ordered as a prospective, also Hurd. At least, I got three of them lined up but for what I couldn't say. I envy you your command but am told I am too late; I hate to think of sitting here for 18 months and then going to San Diego for a shore-sea job although it is submarines and near home.

All the boats have 20MM now, two on all fleet boats with Wahoo adding a third one. Argonaut and N boats have four to six.

The latest figures are 997,441 sunk and 470,283 tons damaged.

Trust you will accept this in lieu of a reply from Reilly.

Ed.

E.K. Swinburne

Commander E.K. Walker,
U.S.S. MAYRANT,
Care of Fleet Post Office,
New York, N. Y.

Say good bye to our biggest (Argonaut). Gilmore was killed in a gun battle in which he did some ramming. Ship is returning to B with Schade in command. Our boats are doing ok.
EKS

Index

to

Series of Taped Interviews

with

Rear Admiral Edward K. Walker, USN (Retired)

Alcohol
    Prohibition observed at Naval Academy in early 1920s, pp. 42-43; smuggling liquor on board the USS Utah (BB-31) in mid-1920s, p. 50

Alton, USS (IX-5)
    Former cruiser Chicago which was a station ship at Pearl Harbor in the early 1930s, p. 74

Antarctic
    Walker's experiences as commanding officer of USS Canisteo (AO-99) during Operation Highjump in 1946-47, pp. 250-258

Arma Corporation
    Built Mark 1 torpedo fire control system in 1930s, p. 117

Army, U.S.
    Army nurses on board the destroyer Mayrant (DD-402) in the Mediterranean in early 1943, p. 214

Asdic
    British term for sonar developed by Allied Submarine Detection Investigation Committee, pp. 143-144

AT & T
    Development of electronic main battery fire control director in 1940s, p. 238

Athletics
    Light heavyweight Ernie Schaaf boxed for the USS Florida (BB-30) in the late 1920s, pp. 59-60

Battleships
    USS Delaware (BB-28) on midshipman cruise in 1922, pp. 24-26; North Dakota (BB-29) on cruise in 1923, pp. 26-27, 29; New York (BB-34) on cruise in 1924, pp. 27-30; living conditions on board the USS Utah (BB-31) and USS Florida (BB-30) in the mid-1920s, pp. 47-48; Utah operations in the Atlantic, pp. 49-51; smuggling of alcohol, pp. 50-51; conversion of the Utah and Florida in the mid-1920s from coal to oil, pp. 54-56; life on board the Florida in late 1920s, pp. 59-61

Beaver, USS (AS-5)
    In mid-1930s, serviced S-boats in Hawaii, pp. 102, 140

Beck, Lieutenant Commander Edward L., USN   (USNA, 1925)
    Commanding officer of the destroyer Phelps (DD-360) at the time of Japanese attack on Pearl Harbor in 1941, pp. 170-172

Bennehoff, Lieutenant Commander Olton R., USN   (USNA, 1918)
    Early work on submarine torpedo fire control systems in the
    mid-1930s, pp. 117-118

Boilers
    Conversion of the USS Utah (BB-31) and Florida (BB-30) from
    coal-burning to oil in the mid-1920s, pp. 54-56; operation of
    the ships' boilers, pp. 57-58

Bonney, Lieutenant Carroll T., USN   (USNA, 1920)
    Instructor at submarine school in mid-1920s, p. 69

Boxing
    Light heavyweight Ernie Schaaf fought for the USS Florida
    (BB-30) in the late 1920s, pp. 59-60

Boyd, Captain David F., Jr., USN   (USNA, 1897)
    Skipper of USS Florida (BB-30) in the mid-1920s, p. 60

Brazil
    Visited by ships of Operation Highjump in early 1947, pp. 252-
    253, 260

Bureau of Ordnance
    Walker began work on torpedo fire control at the bureau in
    1934, pp. 116-118; testing in 1938, pp. 119-120; development
    of torpedo data computer, pp. 120-125, 148; elimination of
    initial bugs in the system, pp. 125-130; erratic torpedoes in
    the early 1940s, pp. 131-132; frugal with funds prior to World
    War II, pp. 132-133; little interest in sound gear before
    World War II, pp. 143-145; Walker's work as an inspector of
    ordnance at various manufacturing companies on Long Island,
    1943-1945, pp. 234-244; operated the Naval Mine Depot at
    Yorktown, Virginia, in the early 1950s, pp. 282, 285-293

Burke, Lieutenant Commander Arleigh A. Burke, USN   (USNA, 1923)
    Development of destroyer torpedo fire control system shortly
    before World War II, pp. 124-125

Canisteo, USS (AO-99)
    Oiler which supported Operation Highjump to Antarctica in
    1946-47, pp. 250-256

Carney, Lieutenant Robert B. "Mick", USN   (USNA, 1916)
    As navigation instructor at Naval Academy in 1924, pp. 27-28

Casablanca
    Role of the USS Mayrant (DD-402) in the invasion of North
    Africa in November 1942, pp. 199-202, 208-209

Chicago, USS (CL-14)
   See Alton, USS (IX-5)

Coal
   Used for firing battleship boilers in the early 1920s, pp. 26, 30

Communications
   Walker, as Pacific Fleet submarine force operations officer, was not aware of U.S. codebreaking and Ultra intercepts until May 1942, pp. 174-176

Cuba
   Alcohol smuggled aboard the USS Utah (BB-31) at Guantanamo Bay, Cuba, in the mid-1920s, pp. 50-51

Decommissioning
   Inactivation of submarines at Philadelphia in the 1930s, pp. 94-96

Delaware, USS (BB-28)
   In midshipman practice squadron in the summer of 1922, pp. 24-25; gunnery practice, pp. 25-26

Destroyers
   Walker had no previous experience in destroyers when he took command of the USS Mayrant (DD-402) in 1942, p. 63; new torpedo fire control system shortly before World War II, pp. 124-125
   See also: Mayrant; Destroyer Squadron Eight; Destroyer Squadron 14

Destroyer Squadron 14
   Operations in the Atlantic in the early 1950s, pp. 273-281; escort of the liner United States into New York during her first trip in 1952, pp. 276-278, 283-284; Walker ordered to command, p. 274

Destroyer Squadron Eight
   Involved in invasion of North Africa in November 1942, pp. 199-203

Diesel Engines
   NELSECO engines in submarines in 1920s and 1930s, pp. 80-81, 107-108

Drinking
   See: Liquor

Dufek, Captain George J., USN (USNA, 1925)
    As commander of a task group for Operation Highjump in Antarctica and trip to Brazil, 1946-47, pp. 251-253

Education
    In Portland, Maine, public schools, 1910-20, pp. 1-2, 7-9
    See also: Naval Academy, U.S.; Naval Postgraduate School

Effingham, USS (APA-165)
    Walker as commanding officer in 1945-46, pp. 244-250

Elokomin, USS (AO-55)
    Fleet oiler commanded briefly by Walker in 1946, p. 250

Engineering Plants
    USS Florida (BB-30) conversion from coal to oil in the mid-1920s, pp. 54-56; operation of battleship boilers, pp. 57-58
    See also: Coal; Diesel Engines

English, Rear Admiral Robert H., USN (USNA, 1911)
    Walker's assessment of as Pacific Fleet submarine force commander in 1942, p. 182; and submarine disposition at Midway, pp. 188-189, 195; killed with staff in plane crash in 1943, pp. 196-197

Escape from Submarines
    Early escape devices, around 1930, were primitive, pp. 71-72; training in escape tank at New London, Connecticut, in 1930s, pp. 103-105

Family Life
    The Navy made little provision for moving men's families in the 1920s and 1930s, pp. 98-100; Mrs. Walker's difficulties getting to Hawaii in 1941, p. 156; Walker's son saved from drowning by Red Ramage in 1941, pp. 157-159; Walker's son as Naval Academy midshipman in early 1950s, pp. 271-272

Fire Control
    Approach practice for firing torpedoes by the submarine R-8 (SS-85) in the early 1930s, pp. 89-91; Walker began work on torpedo fire control at the Bureau of Ordnance in 1934, pp. 116-118; Mark 1 torpedo fire control system tested in 1938, pp. 119-120; development of torpedo data computer, pp. 120-125, 148; system for destroyer torpedoes, pp. 124-125; initial bugs in torpedo data computer worked out, pp. 125-130; commitment of funds in late 1930s to develop fire control radar, pp. 133-134; U.S. torpedo data computer much better than foreign counterparts in World War II, pp. 147-148; testing of Mark 2 system in the Tambor (SS-198) in 1939, pp. 126, 149-151

Florida, USS (BB-30)
    Conversion from coal to oil in mid-1920s, pp. 54-56; operation of engineering plant, pp. 57-58; Commander Claude B. Mayo as exec in 1926, p. 58; crew member Ernie Schaaf as boxer, pp. 59-60; operations in the Atlantic in 1926-27, pp. 60-61

Food
    Primitive storage conditions in submarines in the early 1930s, pp. 75-76; limited amount available for underway periods in the R-8 (SS-85) in the early 1930s, pp. 86-87

Ford Instrument Company
    Walker observes work in gunfire control systems in 1934, p. 117; built Mark 2 torpedo fire control system in late 1930s, p. 126; manufacturer of ordnance components in World War II, p. 235

Fournon, L.R.
    French professor at Naval Academy in 1920s, p. 21

France
    Visited by Naval Academy midshipmen on cruise in 1924, pp. 29-30; defense at Casablanca in November 1942, p. 201

French Frigate Shoals
    Defense of in 1937 naval exercise, pp. 140-141

Friedell, Rear Admiral Wilhelm L., USN   (USNA, 1905)
    Father figure as submarine force commander shortly before World War II, p. 164

Graubert, Captain Arthur H., USN   (USNA, 1925)
    Classmate of Walker's, p. 35

Guantanamo Bay, Cuba
    Alcohol smuggled aboard the USS Utah (BB-31) in mid-1920s, pp. 50-51

Gudgeon, USS (SS-211)
    Guided by Ultra to Japanese submarine in January 1942, pp. 185-186

Gunfire - Naval
    Turret operation in the battleship Delaware (BB-28) in 1922, p. 25; 3-inch guns in submarines in the early 1930s, pp. 76-77; Walker considers guns to be of little value in submarines, pp. 135-136

Gunther, Lieutenant L. Everett, USN (USNA, 1926)
    Submarine force flag lieutenant at the time of the Japanese attack on Pearl Harbor in 1941, pp. 170-172

Haiti
    U.S. sailors on liberty in mid-1920s, pp. 49-50

Hancock, H. Irving
    Author of four novels on the Naval Academy, published 1910-11, p. 6

Hashimoto, Lieutenant Commander Mochitsura, Imperial Japanese Navy
    Transported to Japan by Walker in USS *Effingham* (APA-165) in early 1946, pp. 245-247

Hawaii
    Pleasant living conditions in early 1930s, pp. 87-89; submarine operations in the mid-1930s, p. 140; observations of changes from 1920s to 1970s, p. 157; as a place to raise children, pp. 157-159
    See also: Pearl Harbor

Hazing
    At Naval Academy in the early 1920s, pp. 12-14

Henty, George A.
    English author of adventure novels in the 19th century, p. 15

Herrmann, Rear Admiral, USN (USNA, 1919)
    As superintendent of Naval Postgraduate School in early 1950s, p. 115

Highjump, Operation
    Exploration of Antarctica by the Navy in 1946-47, supported by the oiler *Canisteo* (AO-99), pp. 250-258

Household Goods
    The Navy made little provision for moving men's families in the 1920s and 1930s, pp. 98-100

Hussey, Rear Admiral George F., Jr., USN (USNA, 1916)
    As chief of the Bureau of Ordnance in World War II, pp. 242-243

IBM
    Builder of Mark I antiaircraft computer in World War II, pp. 236-237

Icebergs
    Encountered off Antarctica during Operation Highjump in 1946-47, pp. 254-256

Ice Makers
    Introduced around 1929 in R-boats, p. 75

Indianapolis, USS (CA-35)
    Japanese submarine skipper who sank this cruiser was transported to Japan in early 1946, pp. 245-246

Ingersoll, Vice Admiral Stuart H., USN (USNA, 1921)
    Lived in same house as Walker in 1930s, pp. 2-3; nickname "Slim," p. 3

Inspections
    USS Richmond (CL-9) made grand tour in late 1940 so force commander could inspect submarines, pp. 155-156, 161-162, 167-168; Walker as ordnance inspector at companies on Long Island in World War II, pp. 234-244

Instruction
    Method of instruction at Naval Academy, pp. 23-24; importance of studying English, pp. 34-35

Intelligence
    See: Ultra

"Is-was"
    Device used for setting course and angle of target in submarines before World War II, p. 89

Junkers Ju-88 bombers
    German planes which damaged the destroyer Mayrant (DD-402) in July 1943, pp. 217-219

Kidd, Rear Admiral Isaac C., USN (USNA, 1906)
    Executive officer in USS Utah in mid-1920s, later killed at Pearl Harbor, p. 64

King, Admiral Ernest J., USN (USNA, 1901)
    Commanding officer at submarine school in 1920s, p. 69; expressed appreciation to Walker for fine work done on S-21 in 1937 exercise, p. 141

Kitts, Commander Willard A. III, USN (USNA, 1916)
    Work in Bureau of Ordnance shortly before World War II, pp. 130, 131, 133-134

Korea
    Great mound of captured brassware between Inchon and Seoul in 1946, p. 248

Lawe, William C., USS (DD-763)
    Walker's flagship as commander of Destroyer Squadron 14 in 1951-52, pp. 274, 277

Liquor
　　Prohibition observed at the Naval Academy in the early 1920s, pp. 42-43; smuggling on board the USS Utah (BB-31) in mid-1920s, pp. 50-51

Lockwood, Commander Charles A., Jr., USN (USNA, 1912)
　　Recommends Walker as gunnery and torpedo officer of submarine force in 1940, p. 153; aggressive chief of staff, pp. 164-165

Magruder, Lieutenant Commander Cary W. "Red", USN (USNA, 1908)
　　As a tough duty officer at the Naval Academy in the early 1920s, pp. 17-18

Maintenance
　　Upkeep of submarine diesel engines in the early 1930s, pp. 80-81; inactivation of submarines at Philadelphia in the 1930s, pp. 94-96

Makin Island
　　Raid by Marines under Evans Carlson in mid-August 1942, pp. 177-179

Malta
　　Site of repairs to the destroyer Mayrant (DD-402) in 1943, pp. 223-224, 226, 227

Massachusetts, USS (BB-59)
　　Supported invasion of North Africa in November 1942, pp. 199-201

Massachusetts Institute of Technology
　　Course about gasoline engines in 1925, pp. 45-46

Mayo, Commander Claude B. "Ditty Box", USN (USNA, 1906)
　　As executive officer in the USS Florida (BB-30) in mid-1920s, p. 58

Mayrant, USS (DD-402)
　　Damaged by near-miss German bomb off Sicily in July 1943, pp. 105-106; Walker took command in September 1942 with no prior destroyer experience, pp. 63, 198-199, 209-211; involved in the Allied invasion of North Africa in November 1942, pp. 199-202, 208-209; description of ship's officers, p. 203, 228-229; at Safi, Morocco, in early 1943, pp. 204-206; Walker slept on the bridge while under way, pp. 211-212; at New York Navy Yard in early 1943, pp. 212-213, 230-231; convoys around North Africa in early 1943, pp. 213-214; damaged during support of the invasion of Sicily in 1943, pp. 216-222; repairs of ship at Malta, p. 223

Mediterranean Sea
    See: Malta, North Africa, Sicily

Midway, Battle of
    Disposition of U.S. submarines for the battle in June 1942, pp. 176-177, 188-189; failure of the Tambor to give a complete report on contacts after battle, p. 195

Miller, John Mendelssohn, USN (USNA, 1925)
    Walker's roommate at Naval Academy, p. 12

Mine Depot, Naval
    See: Naval Mine Depot, Yorktown, Virginia

Minelaying
    Purchase of timers for new minelayers in the late 1930s, pp. 124-125; three submarines capable, pp. 177-178; considerations in mine placement, p. 180

Minesweepers
    The USS Skill (AM-115) and USS Strive (AM-117) provided aid to the destroyer Mayrant (DD-402) after she was damaged off Sicily in July 1943, pp. 217-219

Momsen, Lieutenant Charles B., USN (USNA, 1920)
    Inventor of Momsen lung, pp. 103-104

Momsen Lung
    Rescue breathing device for submariners, pp. 71, 103-105

Moon, Captain Don P., USN (USNA, 1916)
    Difficult to work for as destroyer squadron commander in late 1942, pp. 199-200, 215, 231

Morocco
    Invasion of Casablanca in November 1942, pp. 199-202, 208; social engagements at Safi in early 1943, pp. 204-206

Mumma, Lieutenant Morton C., Jr., USN (USNA, 1925)
    Walker's assessment of as skipper of the Sailfish (SS-192) early in World War II, pp. 168-169

Murphy, Lieutenant Commander John W., Jr., USN (USNA, 1925)
    Commanding officer of the USS Tambor (SS-198) in the Battle of Midway, pp. 195-196

Naquin, Lieutenant Oliver F., USN (USNA, 1925)
    Walker's assessment of Squalus (SS-192) skipper, pp. 168-169

Nautilus, USS (SS-168)
   Large U.S. submarine which sank the Japanese carrier Soryu in the Battle of Midway in June 1942, pp. 176-177

Naval Academy, U.S.
   Physical exams in 1921, pp. 2, 10-11; political appointment for Walker in 1921, pp. 7, 10; plebe summer in 1921, pp. 11-14; hazing, pp. 12-14; class standings, pp. 15, 41-42; course work in the early 1920s, pp. 15-16, 23-24, 34-35; midshipmen subjected duty officer Cary Magruder to silence in messhall, pp. 17-19; Rear Admiral Henry B. Wilson as Superintendent, p. 19; Midshipman L.R. Smith drowned during ring baptism ceremony in May 1924, pp. 20-21; influential professors, pp. 21-23; summer cruises in early 1920s, pp. 24-31; social life for midshipmen, pp. 32-33, 40; midshipmen who were friends of Walker in the early 1920s, pp. 35-37; aptitude for service grades, pp. 37-38; spending money for midshipmen, pp. 39-40; graduation in June 1925, p. 41; drinking and smoking by midshipmen, pp. 42-43

Naval Mine Depot, Yorktown, Virginia
   Commanded by Walker, 1952-55, pp. 282, 285-293

Naval Postgraduate School
   General line course in 1932-33, pp. 109-112; Walker's study of ordnance engineering from 1933 to 1935, pp. 112-117; Walker as head of ordnance department, 1947-51, pp. 261-273; move to West Coast in late 1940s, pp. 268-269

Naval War College
   Held in low repute by many officers in the 1930s, pp. 111-112

NELSECO [New London Ship and Engine Company]
   Diesel engines used in submarines in the early 1930s, pp. 80-81. See also: Diesel Engines

New York, USS (BB-34)
   On midshipman cruise to Europe in 1924, pp. 27-30; living conditions, p. 48

New York Navy Yard
   Franklin D. Roosevelt, Jr., fell asleep in telephone booth when his ship was about to leave in March 1943, pp. 212-213; USS Mayrant (DD-402) collision with a buoy in early 1943, pp. 230-231

Nimitz, Admiral Chester W., USN (USNA, 1905)
   Pacific Fleet commander in chief involved in disposition of submarines for the Battle of Midway in June 1942, pp. 176-177; limited role overall in submarine operations, pp. 183-184

North Africa
　　Role of the USS Mayrant (DD-402) in November 1942 invasion, pp. 199-202, 208-209; social engagements involving Lieutenant Franklin D. Roosevelt, Jr., in early 1943, pp. 204-206; Mayrant convoys in early 1943, pp. 213-214

North Dakota, USS (BB-29)
　　On midshipman's cruise to northern Europe in 1923, pp. 26-27, 29

Nurses
　　Army nurses on board the destroyer Mayrant (DD-402) in the Mediterranean in early 1943, p. 214

O-12, USS (SS-73)
　　Converted around 1930 for use in the Arctic, p. 95

Oil
　　Conversion of the battleships Florida (BB-30) and Utah (BB-31) from coal in the mid-1920s, pp. 54-56; fuel in NELSECO diesel engines in the early 1930s, pp. 80-81

Omaha, USS (CL-4)
　　Ran aground in the Bahamas in July 1937, pp. 118-119

Ordnance, Bureau of
　　See: Bureau of Ordnance

Ordnance Engineering
　　Considered most prestigious postgraduate specialty in the Navy in the 1930s, pp. 112-113; program of education from 1947 to 1951 when Walker was ordnance curriculum officer at the Naval Postgraduate School, pp. 261-273
　　See also: Fire Control

Pan American World Airways
　　Long Clipper ride from North Africa to Brazil to New York in 1943, pp. 224-225

Parker, Vice Admiral Edward N. "Butch", USN (USNA, 1925)
　　Classmate of Walker's, pp. 35-36; origin of nickname "Cherub," p. 37

Patton, Lieutenant General George S., Jr., U.S. Army (USMA, 1909)
　　Flamboyant during operation in Sicily in 1943, pp. 222-223

Pay and Allowances
　　Until World War II only enlisted men received extra pay for serving in submarines, p. 68; pay cuts for Navymen in early 1930s, p. 88

Pearl Harbor
    Walker's experiences during the Japanese attack in December 1941, pp. 170-172

Portsmouth Navy Yard
    Site of Naval Academy physical examination, p. 2; Walker's experiences during examination, pp. 10-11

Postgraduate School
    See: Naval Postgraduate School

Prohibition
    At Naval Academy in early 1920s, pp. 42-43; loading liquor on board USS Utah (BB-31), pp. 50-51

R-8, USS (SS-85)
    Conditions on board while operating around Hawaii in the early 1930s, pp. 72-73, 75-77, 79, 83, 86; description of enlisted crew members, pp. 77-79; NELSECO diesel engines for propulsion, pp. 80-81; approach practice for firing torpedoes, pp. 89-91

R-13, USS (SS-90)
    Submarine school boat at New London, Connecticut, in the early 1930s, pp. 92-93, 97, 106-107

Radar
    Commander Willard Kitts committed money for radar development prior to World War II, pp. 133-134

Radio
    Submarine S-21 (SS-126) had a very capable radioman in mid-1930s, p. 82; Walker, as Pacific Fleet submarine force operations officer, was not aware of U.S. codebreaking and Ultra intercepts until May 1942, pp. 174-176

Ramage, Lieutenant Lawson P. "Red", USN (USNA, 1931)
    Rescues Walker's son from undertow in Hawaii in 1941, pp. 158-159

Rescue of Submariners
    Early escape devices, around 1930, were primitive, pp. 71-72; training in escape tank at New London, Connecticut, in 1930s, pp. 103-105

Richmond, USS (CL-9)
    Used as mobile flagship for submarine force commander in 1940-41, pp. 154-156, 161-162, 167-168; staff moved ashore in early 1941, pp. 159-160

Roosevelt, Franklin D.
    Entertained Admiral and Mrs. Walker at White House in 1943 and prepared martinis, pp. 232-233

Roosevelt, Lieutenant Franklin D., Jr., USNR
    Wounded in the USS Mayrant (DD-402) in 1943, p. 106; Walker's assessment of, p. 103; social obligations and experiences with Roosevelt on board, pp. 204-206; temporary disappearance from the Mayrant in March 1943, pp. 212-213; recommended for Silver Star by Walker for helping shipmate during air raid on USS Mayrant in 1943, p. 220; invited to lunch by General Lord Gort in 1943 with Walker, pp. 220-223; wounded in July 1943, p. 218

Roosevelt, Major James "Jimmy", USMCR
    Involved with Walker in planning August 1942 raid on Makin Island, pp. 177-179

S-21, USS (SS-126)
    Walker had separate room as skipper in mid-1930s, p. 79; very capable radioman in the crew, p. 82; serviced by tender Beaver (AS-5) at Hawaii, p. 102; operations out of Pearl Harbor while commanded by Walker from 1935 to 1937, pp. 134-141

S-31, USS (SS-136)
    During Walker's brief command tenure in late 1937, this submarine made a deep dive in the Atlantic and was decommissioned at Philadelphia, pp. 118-119

Safi, Morocco
    See: Morocco

Savadkin, Lieutenant Lawrence, USN
    Engineer officer in the USS Mayrant (DD-402) in 1943, pp. 105-106

Schaaf, Ernie
    Light heavyweight boxer in the USS Florida (BB-30) in mid-1920s, p. 59; death at age 25, p. 60

Schuyler, Captain Garrett L., USN (USNA, 1906)
    Idea man as research division officer at the Bureau of Ordnance around 1940, p. 146

Sexton, Rear Admiral Walton R., USN (USNA, 1897)
    Captain of USS Utah (BB-31) in mid-1920s, p. 51

Sicily
    Operations of the destroyer Mayrant (DD-402) during the invasion of Sicily in the summer of 1943, pp. 216-221

"Slipstick Willie"
  See: Thomson, Earl W.

Smith, Midshipman Leicester R., USN
  Drowned in Dewey Basin in May 1924 during Naval Academy ceremony, pp. 20-21

Smoking
  Rules about at the Naval Academy in the early 1930s, p. 43

Smuggling
  Alcohol put aboard the USS Utah (BB-31) in Cuba in the mid-1920s, pp. 50-51

Snapper, USS (SS-185)
  Submarine used for torpedo fire control tests in late 1938, pp. 119-120, 127, 129, 149-150

Sonar
  In captain's sea cabin in USS Mayrant (DD-402) in World War II, p. 212; See also: Sound Gear

Sound Gear
  Primitive listening devices in submarines in 1920s and 1930s, p. 96; Walker perceived little interest in development by the Bureau of Ordnance in the period around 1940, pp. 143-145

Spangel, Rear Admiral Herman A., USN (USNA, 1914)
  Superintendent of Naval Postgraduate School in late 1940s, p. 263; supervised PG School moving to West Coast, p. 168

Sperry
  Manufacturer of equipment for the Navy in World War II, p. 243

Stroop, Rear Admiral Paul D., USN (USNA, 1926)
  Not selected for ordnance PG in 1930s, later became Chief of the Bureau of Naval Weapons, p. 110

Styer, Commander Charles W., USN (USNA, 1918)
  Walker's assessment of as submarine force staff officer, pp. 165-166

Submariners
  Many U.S. naval officers who went to submarine school in the 1920s were ordered to go, not true volunteers, pp. 53, 62; until World War II, only enlisted men received extra pay for serving in submarines, p. 68; description of enlisted crew members in early 1930s, pp. 77-79; very capable radioman in

the S-21 (SS-126) in the mid-1930s, p. 82; training in escape tank at New London in 1930s, pp. 103-105; process of qualifying for command in 1930s, pp. 107-108; submarine force not considered elite in the Navy until shortly before World War II, pp. 108-109; initially skeptical of torpedo data computer, but later enthusiastic, pp. 125-130; desirable qualities in submarine skippers in the early 1940s, pp. 164, 169-170; submarine squadron and division commanders had a limited role in Pacific operations in World War II, pp. 181-182; Richard Voge, rather than John Murphy, chosen as submarine force operations officer in mid-1942, pp. 195-196; Rear Admiral Robert H. English and staff killed in airplane crash in January 1943, pp. 196-197

Submarines
  Walker's first dive in an O-boat while at submarine school in 1927, p. 65; sinking of the S-51 (SS-162) and S-4 (SS-109) in the 1920s, p. 70; early escape devices for submarines around 1930, pp. 71-72; living conditions in R-boats in the early 1930s, pp. 72-73, 75-76, 86-87; office arrangement ashore for R-boats in Hawaii, pp. 73-74; operation of R-8 (SS-85) in early 1930s, pp. 75-77, 79, 83, 86, 89-91; NELSECO diesel engines, pp. 80-81; R-13 (SS-90) as school boat at New London in early 1930s, pp. 92-93, 97, 106-107; decommissioning of R-boats and S-boats at Philadelphia in 1930s, pp. 94-96; O-12 (SS-73) converted around 1930 for use in the Arctic, p. 95; primitive sound gear in 1920s and 1930s, p. 96; S-boats serviced by tender Beaver (AS-5) at Hawaii in 1930s, p. 102; S-31 (SS-136) decommissioned in 1937 after a deep dive, pp. 118-119; USS Snapper (SS-185) used for torpedo fire control tests in late 1930s, pp. 119-120, 127, 129; S-21 (SS-126) operations out of Pearl Harbor from 1935 to 1937, pp. 134-141; Tambor (SS-198) used to test Mark 2 fire control system in 1939, pp. 126, 149-151; Walker's service as gunnery and torpedo officer on the submarine force staff in 1940-41, pp. 154-166; as operations officer, 1941-42, pp. 166-197; advantages of fleet boats over predecessors, p. 163; disposition of U.S. submarines for the Battle of Midway in June 1942, p. 176; work with other U.S. warships, pp. 190-191; Walker the originator of "down-the-throat" torpedo shot, pp. 193-194; See also: Fire Control; Torpedoes

Submarine School
  Instruction during mid-1920s, pp. 52, 65-67, 69-70

Swinburne, Captain Edwin R., USN (USNA, 1925)
  Notified Walker of attack on Pearl Harbor, p. 170; letter to Walker, dated February 1943, is an appendix to Walker's oral history volume.

Tambor, USS (SS-198)
    Submarine outfitted with Mark 2 torpedo fire control system in 1939, pp. 126, 149-151; failure to supply full contact report after the Battle of Midway in June 1942, p. 195

Taylor, Commander Edwin A., USN (USNA, 1922)
    As commanding officer of the USS Mayrant (DD-402) early in World War II, p. 210

Thomson, Earl W.
    Professor known as "Slipstick Willie" at Naval Academy in the early 1920s, p. 23

Tobacco
    Rules about smoking at the Naval Academy in the early 1920s, p. 43

Torpedo Data Computer
    Developed in the Bureau of Ordnance in the late 1930s, pp. 120-125, 148; improved to work out initial bugs, pp. 125-132

Torpedoes
    Approach practice for torpedo firing by the R-8 (SS-85) in the early 1930s, pp. 89-91; early work on submarine torpedo fire control system at the Bureau of Ordnance in the mid-1930s, pp. 116-118; Mark 1 fire control system tested in 1938, pp. 119-120; development of torpedo data computer shortly before World War II, pp. 120-125, 148; destroyer fire control system, pp. 124-125; bugs worked out of system and initial skepticism overcome, pp. 125-130; difficulties with malfunctioning torpedoes in early 1940s, pp. 131-132, 151-153, 189

Training
    See: Submarine School

Turrets
    Tight clearance in 12-inch gun turret in USS Delaware (BB-28) in 1922, pp. 25-26

Ultra
    Walker not aware of this codebreaking system until May 1942, pp. 174-176; used to guide the Gudgeon (SS-211) to a Japanese submarine in January 1942, pp. 185=186

Uniforms
    Officers had to maintain a large supply of uniforms in the 1920s and 1930s, pp. 100-101

United States, SS
    Escorted on maiden voyage into New York in 1952 by ships of DesRon 14, pp. 277-278

Utah, USS (BB-31)
    Operated out of Boston to the Caribbean in 1920s, no flag quarters on board, pp. 47-51; Commander Isaac C. Kidd as exec in mid-1920s, p. 64

Van Valkenburgh, Lieutenant Commander Franklin, USN (USNA, 1909)
    Entertained midshipmen as instructor at Naval Academy in early 1920s, p. 32

Voge, Lieutenant Commander Richard G., USN (USNA, 1925)
    Became submarine force operations officer in mid-1942, pp. 195-196

Wake
    U.S. submarine patrols to this mid-Pacific island in late 1941, p. 173

Walker, Rear Admiral Edward K., USN
    Early education, pp. 1-2, 7-9; memories of World War I, pp. 3-5; celebration of Armistice Day, November 11, 1918, p. 5; desire to go to Naval Academy instilled by H. Irving Hancock's series of novels for boys, p. 6; appointment to Naval Academy, pp. 2, 7, 10; plebe summer, pp. 11-14; favorite books as midshipman, p. 13; victim of hazing at Naval Academy, pp. 12, 14; course work at Naval Academy, pp. 15-16, 23-24; class standings, pp. 15, 41-42; midshipmen's cruises, pp. 24-31; social life as midshipman, pp. 32-33, 40; duty on board the USS Florida (BB-30), pp. 54-55, 57-61; recollections of submarine school, pp. 65-66, 69-70; duty in USS R-8 (SS-85), pp. 72-92, 96; sent to PG School for general line course in 1932, pp. 109-116; ordered to Bureau of Ordnance in 1934, p. 116; development of torpedo fire control equipment at Bureau of Ordnance in late 1930s, pp. 116-133, 141-151; recollections of December 7, 1941, pp. 170-172; involvement in planning Makin Island raid, pp. 177-179; originator of "down-the-throat" shot in early 1940s, pp. 193-194; command of USS Mayrant (DD-402) in 1942-43, pp. 105-106, 198-223, 226-231; naval inspector at various companies on Long Island, 1943-45, pp. 234-244; commanding officer of USS Effingham (APA-165), 1945-46, p. 246; Lieutenant Commander Hashimoto back to Japan after interrogations on USS Effingham, pp. 245-247; commanding officer of USS Elokomin (AO-55) in 1946, p. 250; as commanding officer of USS Canisteo in 1946-47, pp. 250-261; department head at Naval Postgraduate School, 1947-1951, pp. 261-273; as

Commander Destroyer Squadron 14 in 1951-52, pp. 273-281, 283-284; escorting the SS United States on maiden voyage into New York, pp. 177-178; command of naval mine depot at Yorktown, pp. 282, 285-293; civilian activities following retirement from active naval service, pp. 294-299

Walker, Rear Admiral Edward K., Jr., SC, USN (USNA, 1954)
Saved from drowning in 1941 by Red Ramage, pp. 157-159; as a Naval Academy midshipman in the early 1950s, pp. 271-272, 288; as a naval officer, pp. 297-298

Walker, Miriam Whitmore
Meets and marries E.K. Walker in 1920s, pp. 43-45, 52; difficulties getting to Hawaii in 1941, p. 156

War College
See: Naval War College

Watson Elevator Company
Manufacturer of target bearing indicators for submarines in World War II, p. 235

Watson, Thomas J.
As head of International Business Machines in the 1940s, pp. 236-237

Wellborn, Captain Charles, Jr., USN (USNA, 1921)
As Commander Destroyer Squadron Eight in 1943, pp. 214-215

Will, Lieutenant Commander John M., "Dutch", USN (USNA, 1923)
Inspection of tender as submarine force staff officer in 1941, p. 66

Wilson, Rear Admiral Henry B., USN (USNA, 1881)
Father figure as Superintendent of the Naval Academy, July 1921-February 1925, p. 19; rules concerning smoking at Naval Academy in early 1920s, p. 43

Withers, Rear Admiral Thomas, USN (USNA, 1906)
Walker's assessment of, pp. 165, 182; set up rest program for submariners, pp. 173-174; relationship with Admiral Chester Nimitz, p. 183

World War II
Difficulties with U.S. submarine torpedoes early in the war, pp. 131-132, 151-153, 189; Japanese attack on Pearl Harbor in December 1941, pp. 170-172; Walker learns of Ultra codebreaking capability in May 1942, pp. 74-176; disposition

of submarines for the Battle of Midway in June 1942, pp. 176-177, 188-189; planning for the use of submarines in the August 1942 raid at Makin Island, pp. 177-179; submarine minelaying, p. 180; limited role for submarine squadron and division commanders, pp. 181-182; considerations in U.S. submarine dispositions, pp. 183-185; USS Gudgeon (SS-211) guided by Ultra to Japanese submarine in January 1942, pp. 185-186; loss of Captain John Cromwell in the Sculpin (SS-191) in November 1943, pp. 186-87; interaction between Pacific Fleet submarines and other U.S. warships, pp. 190-191; Walker originated down-the-throat tactic, pp. 193-194; Richard Voge selected as Pacific Fleet submarine force operations officer in mid-1942, pp. 195-196; role of the destroyer Mayrant (DD-402) in the invasion of North Africa in November 1942, pp. 199-202, 208-209; damaged during support of the invasion of Sicily in 1943, pp. 216-222; Walker's service as inspector of ordnance on Long Island, 1943-45, pp. 234-244

Yorktown, Virginia
    See: Naval Mine Depot, Yorktown, Virginia